BIRCHBARK CANOE

BIRCHBARK CANOE

◆ ■ ◆

Living Among the Algonquin

DAVID GIDMARK

FIREFLY BOOKS

A FIREFLY BOOK

Published by Firefly Books Ltd. 1997

2nd printing, 2023

Library of Congress Control Number: 2023947042

Library and Archives Canada Cataloguing in Publication
Title: Birchbark canoe : living among the Algonquin / David Gidmark.
Names: Gidmark, David, author.
Description: Includes index. | Previously published: Willowdale, Ontario: Firefly Books, 1997.
Identifiers: Canadiana 20230545009 | ISBN 9780228104773 (softcover)
Subjects: CSH: First Nations—Boats—Québec (Province) | LCSH: Canoes and canoeing. | LCSH: Boatbuilding. | CSH: First Nations—Boats—Québec (Province) | CSH: First Nations—Québec (Province)
Classification: LCC E99.A349 G48 2024 | DDC 970.004/973—dc23

Published in Canada by
Firefly Books Ltd.
50 Staples Avenue, Unit 1
Richmond Hill, Ontario L4B 0A7

Published in the United States by
Firefly Books (U.S.) Inc.
P.O. Box 1338, Ellicott Station
Buffalo, New York 14205

Design by Counterpunch/Linda Gustafson
Production by Denise Schon Books Inc.

Printed in China | E

Canada

We acknowledge the support of the Government of Canada.

FSC
www.fsc.org
MIX
Paper from
responsible sources
FSC® C160794

Opening page photo: Abitibi, western Quebec, c. 1910.

Dedicated to
Patrick Maranda
(1901–1987)
a maker of superlative birchbark canoes

and to two Algonquin birchbark canoe makers
who were both gentlemen and gentle men:

Jocko Carle
(1910–1981)

Basil Smith
(1911–1997)

When the sky shall be no longer blue and fair, and brooks shall cease to sing the song of summer, and lordly moose no longer tear the lily from its bed of mud, and lusty trout no longer flirt and jump for very love of living; when smiling birch and somber spruce, and all nature, shall break their spell and cease to beckon, then, but not till then, shall I no longer love the birch canoe.

— Edwin Tappan Adney, 1900

CHAPTER 1

Two herring gulls swooped back and forth over us screaming, "Hiyah! hiyah! hiyah!" They were looking for fish and so were we.

We spotted a net set for whitefish in the channel between Sand Island off the Bayfield Peninsula in Lake Superior and the mainland. A fishing boat had just come to attend to it. Commercial fishing flourishes in the pristine, cold, deep waters of the world's greatest lake. The owner of the general store in Port Wing, Wisconsin, is a commercial fisherman. He sells fresh trout, whitefish, and herring almost daily, fish that he smokes himself all the time.

It was a Huckleberry Finn trip we were making in the summer of 1976 in a rowboat on Lake Superior. My cousin Tim and I had borrowed the boat in Port Wing, and we were rowing up to the Apostle Islands a few days' journey away. I rowed; I needed the exercise more than Tim, and I have always enjoyed the lusty activity of rowing. It was not an aerobic exercise at the speed I maintained, but there was nevertheless the clear feeling that the rhythmic pulling on the oars expanded the lungs as much as it worked the latissimus dorsi muscles.

We approached the fisherman come to retrieve his whitefish. "Would you have a fish you could sell us?" I asked him, just as he started to pull the net aboard.

"I might have," he said, removing a fish that must have weighed close to three pounds from his net. "This do?"

"It'll be more than enough," I answered. "How much do we owe you?"

"A couple of dollars will be fine," he said, establishing in my mind once again that it's much better to deal with the supplier.

I didn't carry a billfold in those days, so I looked around the boat for my shirt and removed two dollar bills from one of the pockets. I handed the money to the man with one hand and reached for the fish with the other. The fish was still alive, and to dispatch it I wielded the oar awkwardly. The man had made what certainly must have been one of his more unusual sales. We rowed off.

Sometimes when one is involved in an activity one is conscious of that activity in the context of future time. We were in our late twenties, but we were living the summer dreams of young boys. "I was rich, if not in money, in sunny hours and summer days, and spent them lavishly," wrote Thoreau. I thought of the future, and I hoped that I would forever have time for such carefree trips as this.

It was early July and the lake was cold even if the air was warm. Hypothermia can overcome people in five minutes, and even lead to death in a short time. Lake Superior is a dangerous lake, for the water is always near freezing in the depths. Surface water can be very warm in the middle of the summer. Then the wind and currents can bring frigid water quickly to any part of the lake. Despite the cold water, Tim doffed his clothes and jumped from the boat to swim leisurely behind as I continued to row. In good shape, he was nevertheless a little adipose and thus somewhat protected against hypothermia.

We put ashore to look for a camping spot on the beach. One of the best-kept secrets of North America is the beauty of Lake Superior and the ease with which an idyllic camping spot — totally free of other people, not to mention camping fees — may be found. Piles of driftwood from the lake are always at hand, the dry wood superb for starting a fire. We quickly fried up fish and potatoes.

As we slept on the shore that night, we were lulled to sleep by the special rhythm of Lake Superior, a lapping of the waves on the shore that tells one clearly that he is not by the ocean or a smaller inland lake.

The next day we found one of the first outposts of civilization we had seen on the trip — a tavern located on the shore of Lake Superior. We put ashore and for a few hours partook of some of civilization's more dispensable amenities.

While we were there, one of the local people mentioned that a group of Chippewa was offering a class in birchbark canoe making not far away. The Chippewa (called Ojibway in Canada) were from the Red Cliff Reservation some distance away, but the classes were being held at Raspberry Bay, a campground only about four miles from where we were.

"Let's go see that," I said to Tim. Fortunately, his interest in the canoe building surpassed his interest in the tavern, but I wasn't sure how long the Indian cultural event would win out. He had a deep appreciation for alcohol in all its forms, with the possible exception of rubbing alcohol.

We camped that night on the lakeshore. Over a hot driftwood fire and not a little beer, we made a game attempt at solving a number of the world's problems, at coming up with ideas about how such poor prospects as ourselves could meet pretty young women. We didn't want to meet women worthy of us; we were fussier than that. And most of all, woven through our talk, blustery and otherwise, was our deep appreciation of this great lake.

As if in some kind of natural synchronicity, the fire waned as the northern lights waxed. They started as they often do: an early, white arc in the north that became differentiated into multicoloured beams that played back and forth across the heavens. The fire had nearly gone out by this time, but it continued to provide some light. On a hunch, I walked fifty feet away from the fire and looked to the north over the mirrorlike surface of the lake. The lake *was* a mirror, for I could see the beams of light from the north — their colours included — reflected on the surface of the water. I had never seen this before.

The next morning, we left our gear in the woods behind the beach and started out along the four miles of bush road to Raspberry Bay.

The campground was an open area. White pines provided shade. A chipmunk scampered across the ground. Two finches warbled in a nearby tree.

A birchbark canoe was the centre of attention. It was seventeen feet long, with ribs of cedar. The lining was also of cedar. The canoe was covered with sheets of birchbark sewn together with root. Root had also been used to bind the gunwales.

Although there were many Chippewa present, only a couple were learning the construction of a birchbark canoe. Most of the people — children and adults — were preparing a large midsummer picnic. Each of them at one time or another wandered over to take a look at the canoe.

"We had these long ago," said one old Chippewa man. "My father could build them."

"Did you ever learn?" I asked. A thought flashed through my mind: how many skills of my father and my grandfather had I left unlearned?

"No, I never did," said the man. "I should have, maybe. Never did though."

It was this same man who later taught me my first lesson in the Indian's concept of time. As I was a little reticent about approaching the Indians – they seemed so shy – I went up to the old man, wondering if he had a watch. "Can you tell me what time it is?" I asked him. I needed to know so that Tim and I could allow ourselves enough time to walk the four miles back to our camp on the lakeshore.

"Oh, I don't know," he said slowly as he raised his head, "about six days since it rained."

I figured we had plenty of time to get back to our camp.

Of the hundred or so people in the camp, only three or four were white. We approached one young white man who seemed to be conducting the class and introduced ourselves.

His name was Ron, and he explained that he was part of a small group headquartered in Iowa dedicated to helping Indians regain lost skills.

"Any chance we could stay around and watch?" I asked.

"Fine with me," he said, "but I'm not the boss. You'll have to ask the chief."

Other people directed us to the chief, a man in his forties.

"Would it be possible for us to watch the people making the birchbark canoe?" I asked. I told him that Ron said it was all right with him. I hoped that would not tip the scales in the wrong direction.

"I suppose," the chief said with a smile. We walked back to where Ron was working. He appeared pleased to have two more students, albeit fairly inactive ones.

His main student was a Chippewa man, slightly younger than Ron, from the reservation at Red Cliff. He was interested in regaining the skill and was attentive to all Ron said.

There was something about this birchbark canoe that was a strong crystallization for me of all that is fascinating in Indian culture – and there is much. It hit me then, and it came to me over and over again in years to come. The effect of that canoe at Lake Superior in 1976 was something I could elucidate only later: the birchbark canoe may be the most striking manifestation of the material culture of the North American Indian.

Tim and I stayed at Raspberry Bay four more days. Morning and evening we walked the four miles to and from our camping spot on Lake Superior. Every day the birchbark canoe was more formed, and every day we became more enchanted with Indian culture. At the time I thought it ironic that Ron, rather than the Chippewa, encouraged our enthusiasm. Later, I realized that the fascinating aspects of Indian culture were perhaps clearer to those who were not a part of it.

Material culture is that part of a culture that is tangible – crafts, more or less. It is well enough to speak of amorphous, mysterious legends or an unfathomable language, but when there is something that one can get one's hands on – the impressive birchbark canoe, for example – the effect is mesmerizing.

I had once before thought semiseriously about the birchbark canoe. It was when I was in northern Quebec working in a logging camp. I had never seen a birchbark canoe, but with bark from some of the trees we were cutting, I made a reasonable facsimile of one. Rather, I should say, a reasonable facsimile of a toy birchbark canoe of the kind that is sold to tourists. Looking at the little foot-long canoe I had made, I thought of the full-size birchbark canoe. Wouldn't it be interesting if someone could make a full-size birchbark canoe and coat the outside with fibreglass so it would last? (This bizarre impression that I had of the birchbark canoe at the time would later pale next to the wild ideas of others I would encounter.)

Ron's ability seemed magic to me. Suppose I wanted to build a birchbark canoe myself; how would I do it?

"Are there any books on the subject?" I asked him.

"There's a very good one," he said. "You can get it from the Smithsonian Institution. It's called *The Bark Canoes and Skin Boats of North America.*"

I wrote down the title, but it seemed inappropriate to me to learn birchbark canoe building from a book.

"Is there any place in North America where Indians still make birchbark canoes?" I asked him.

"Yes," he said. "Maniwaki, in Canada."

I was dumbfounded. For months I had been planning to move from Montreal to the Maniwaki area so that I could pursue my writing career in quiet surroundings. I had been to the town many times and had worked briefly for a lumber company there.

CHAPTER 2

The town of Maniwaki, Quebec, lies in logging country at the edge of the Laurentian Highlands at the confluence of the Désert and Gatineau rivers. Abutting the village is the River Désert Algonquin Reserve. (In Canada, the word *reserve* is used. In the United States the word *reservation* is used.) The River Désert Reserve population is just over one thousand, of which number many are whites married to Indians, making it the largest reserve of the Algonquin nation. The nation is primarily located on slightly less than a dozen reserves in western Quebec and on one in eastern Ontario — Golden Lake. In addition, there are other communities that include a significant number of Algonquin in their population. The total Algonquin population is between five and ten thousand. (The name of the nation is not to be confused with that of the linguistic family, Algonquian, which also refers to other nations, and therefore other Indian languages, that are closely related.)

There may have been people in the Algonquin territory of western Quebec and eastern Ontario as early as 9000 BC, though whether they were Algonquin is difficult to determine. There is some indication

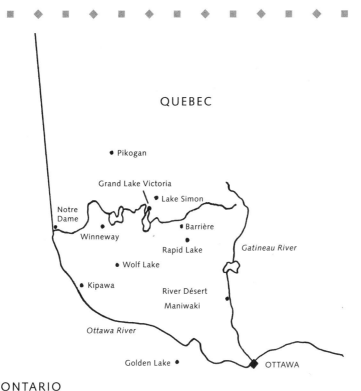

Location of Algonquin communities in western Quebec and eastern Ontario

among the people themselves that the Algonquin came from the east. Samuel de Champlain first met the Algonquin at Tadoussac, east of Quebec City, in 1603. On another voyage, Champlain met various groups of Algonquin on the Ottawa River. One group on Morrison's Island was very important to trade even before the arrival of the Europeans. In excavations there, copper, whalebone, and obsidian have been found. After the arrival of the Europeans, the fur trade supplanted the trade between Natives.

The rowboat trip along the shore of Lake Superior had been a short vacation, but my imagination had been captured by the birchbark canoe I saw there. Ron knew little about the Indian birchbark canoe builder in Maniwaki, only that there was one. I never learned how he had found out about him. I was aware of the reserve in Maniwaki. One

Lumberman's birchbark canoe and lean-to in the late nineteenth century.

goes through it on the southern route into town. I hoped the fact that I knew no one there would not be an impediment to learning more about the birchbark canoe.

When I arrived in Maniwaki, I rented a room in a little river hotel that had served a couple of generations of lumberjacks.

Over a beer I asked the hotelier, an amiable man who had been born in Ireland, about the lumberjacks.

He laughed. "Some of the foremen used to have quite a recruiting technique. The foreman would come by the hotel with a bus. He'd tell the men here that he had a lot of cases of beer. And he wouldn't be lying either. He'd tell them to come out to the bus to look at the beer for themselves. It was the only way they could get men sometimes."

I ordered another beer while the hotel owner continued. "It's quieted down a lot from the old days. When men came out after a few months in the bush, they'd have money to spend and they'd be pretty rambunctious. We had to ban arm wrestling, because they'd no sooner start a friendly match than a fight would break out. Sometimes I'd go through two or three shirts a night breaking up fights."

It was a comfortable little hotel, old as it was. The price of a room, four dollars in 1976, was not at a level that would make one nervous about his finances when moving in.

Over a game of pool I came to know a few local people, including a number of Algonquin from the reserve. The Algonquin language was taught in the schools in town, I soon learned. The Indian children at that time were enrolled in an English elementary school. My interest in that birchbark canoe on the shores of Lake Superior soon grew to a fascination with the entire Native culture in Maniwaki.

The next day I telephoned one of the women who taught the language and asked her about private lessons. She suggested I come by once a week for an hour's lesson.

The woman did not have published materials from which to work, but she had her own lesson plans. "We all write the language in a different way," she said. I had already gathered that there was a significant difference of opinion among the language teachers, with linguists' ideas thrown in for good measure, and I wondered whether the language was structured to a degree or whether speaking, learning, and teaching it was a process full of electives.

Coming face to face with another language is always daunting, especially if one is intending to learn it. When I went to school in France, learning French seemed an ambitious undertaking. Algonquin was an incredible departure.

Nind anicinâbem. Kid anicinâbem. Anicinâbemo. I speak Indian. You speak Indian. He speaks Indian. (*"Anicinabe"* is "Indian." The word for "Algonquin" is *"Omahamiwinini."*)

The language was full of mysteries. I was glad to see that Algonquin had conjugations; at least there was some sort of organization. Later I was to learn how much structure there actually was. There was virtually nothing of the language that could not be figured out in time, in some instances a lot of time. It was very highly systematized; figuring out the system was the key.

Missionary Chrysostom Verwyst of Ashland, Wisconsin, wrote about the Ojibway language in his *Chippewa Exercises* (1901):

> The Chippewa [Ojibway, virtually the same as Algonquin] language is a beautiful language . . . It is the very embodiment of system and regularity. The Chippewa language is a language of terminations. When a person knows a Chippewa root, he yet knows next to nothing, for that root receives almost countless terminations to express all possible modes of being and acting.

It quickly became clear that there were far more differences between Algonquin and English than there were between English and French. Algonquin was much further away from English than even Chinese or Russian. Learning this language was an ambitious undertaking, much more difficult than putting together a birchbark canoe. Many aspects of the Algonquin culture had to be approached with the most profound intellectual humility.

I went to the lessons each week and took home the notes that my teacher provided. I felt I was making good progress, but it soon became evident that I did not yet even understand how difficult the language was.

One day I visited Father Deschênes, the Oblate missionary who was the pastor at what everyone called the Indian church. The Oblates had been among the first colonizers in the Maniwaki area in the middle of the nineteenth century. When the government set up the Algonquin reserve in Maniwaki by moving most of the Algonquin from Oka, near Montreal, the Oblates came along to minister to the spiritual needs of the people.

Father Deschênes, a spare man in his late sixties, invited me into the rectory and showed me some Algonquin language books. He himself spoke Algonquin – it was almost a necessity years ago when the old people knew little English or French – and he spoke Cree, thanks to a long stint in the north.

"Is the Algonquin language really difficult?" I asked.

He only smiled. Then he explained that the early French missionaries had wanted to convert the Algonquin to Christianity, not to the French language. It was more practical for the missionary to learn Algonquin than to wait until his potential flock learned French.

Father Deschênes told me more about the books. They were compiled essentially from Jesuit, Oblate, and Sulpician works dating back to the 1660s. The missionaries had made quite an intellectual investment in their missions to the Indians. Abbot Jean-André Cuoq, a Sulpician, wrote an exclusive lexicon of the Algonquin language in 1886, in which he tried to explain meanings as well as he could with references to Hebrew, German, Dutch, Cree, Abnaki, Iroquois, Ottawa, and Saulteaux. He also wrote an Algonquin grammar in 1891.

In 1907, Georges Lemoine, an Oblate missionary in western Quebec, published a paper entitled "The Genius of the Algonquin Language." This became the preface of his impressive *Dictionnaire Français-Algonquin* in 1909.

In the twentieth century, however, the accent has been on acculturation for its own sake – generally via the English language. Indian children were punished – widely and severely – for speaking Indian. I'm sure Lemoine and Cuoq would have been horrified.

In the seventeenth, eighteenth, nineteenth, and even twentieth centuries, the temporal powers-that-be appear to have placed little or no emphasis on the Indian languages, at least, not to the point of producing dictionaries and grammars, except for some confused, late twentieth-century efforts to play catch-up. Anyone who would learn or teach an Indian language today faces a new, almost insurmountable obstacle – ubiquitous television – which is white culture taken virtually intravenously.

Father Deschênes lent me the Cuoq grammar of Algonquin and I photocopied it. The Lemoine dictionary, published more than seventy years before, was still available, but was buried in the basement of the Oblate seminary in Ottawa. I eventually obtained a copy there and had it bound.

When the missionaries came centuries ago, they had done their work on the Indian language using the Roman alphabet and came up with a way of writing that was clear and practical. It was much easier to pronounce Algonquin than it was to pronounce English or French solely by relying on the Roman alphabet.

The next week, I asked my language tutor if there was an older person on the reserve who might like a boarder. "It would be a good chance for me to learn Algonquin. I'd like to live with someone who can speak it."

She gave me the telephone number of her aunt, a widow by the name of Mrs. Carle. I called, introduced myself, and she invited me over for a visit.

It happened that Mrs. Carle lived close to town and just two houses away from the birchbark canoe maker whom I had not yet met. I had visions at this time of writing and studying Algonquin, and of simply walking a few feet down the road to learn birchbark canoe building. I thought that it promised to be a kind of educational easy street. It turned out to be not quite so simple.

The studying with Mrs. Carle went well, however. She was a quiet-spoken woman in her late sixties. Her husband, Peter, had died in the early 1970s. He had been a birchbark canoe maker, brother of Jocko Carle whom I was later to admire so much. Although Algonquin was Mrs. Carle's first language, she spoke English well. Unlike most of the Indians of her generation in Maniwaki, particularly the men who had worked off the reserve and were trilingual, Mrs. Carle had a limited knowledge of French.

She was exceptionally patient with my attempts to learn Algonquin, and I soon ceased the private lessons with her niece. Mrs. Carle was clear in her explanations of the language. I had the Lemoine dictionary and the Cuoq grammar, and she enjoyed going through the dictionary with me. Many times I would read an Algonquin word from the dictionary and she would recognize it as an old word, one that had been employed many years ago but that had passed out of common usage.

One day I noticed William Commanda, the canoe maker, sitting on his porch watching the traffic passing on the highway to Ottawa. I introduced myself and told him about my interest in his craft. His long hair was held back with a headband decorated in the floral beadwork style of the woodland Indians. He was about five foot eight, quite husky, and I noticed he had no thumb on his left hand. He looked powerful despite his sixty-odd years.

"Come on, I'll show you the birchbark canoe if you want," he said. "It's in the shop."

He opened the door and once again I stood in awe of a birchbark canoe. There, hanging from the ceiling, was a fourteen-foot birchbark canoe. The canoe I had seen weeks earlier on Lake Superior was made out of many sheets of bark sewn together with spruce root. It had taken perhaps eight sheets to cover the canoe. The one I was looking at in Maniwaki was covered with a single sheet of birchbark. I had not even imagined that such a large sheet of bark could be found.

"We always make them out of one piece of birchbark," William said.

I noticed other differences between this canoe and the one I had seen on Lake Superior. The hull of the one on Lake Superior had been formed more or less in the shape of a log. The hull of this one looked like those I had seen on canvas canoes.

I continued to marvel at the canoe. The bottom was essentially flat and well formed, the spruce root sewing pleasing to the eye, and there were bear and fish designs on the bark.

"That's not painted; that's scraped," said William. "This is winter bark. It's dark when you take it off, and that's why you can make designs on it."

On my next visit to William's shop, I asked more questions about the birchbark canoe. He was very free with his information and with social commentary. Meanwhile, I continued my language lessons, gradually increasing my vocabulary.

Then one day, I reasoned the time was right to broach the question that was so important to me.

I had reason to be encouraged. Most of the Indians on the reserve had been open to me. William himself always welcomed my visits. He answered my questions about the canoe, volunteered more information on his own, and always offered his comments about the white man.

Also to be considered was the fact that I was learning the Algonquin language. In the first few months of my study of the language, my vocabulary had increased to nearly five hundred words. I wondered whether my efforts would indicate sincerity to him.

"William," I began with great enthusiasm, "do you suppose that I might come by from time to time and learn how to build a birchbark canoe with you?"

"No," he said, his friendliness tempered with firmness. "I will never teach a white man how to build a birchbark canoe."

There, quite quickly, went all my hopes.

CHAPTER 3

My disappointment in William's not wanting to teach me canoe making did not dampen my enthusiasm for the birchbark canoe.

It is difficult to trace the history of the birchbark canoe prior to European contact. Native oral history is slight in its mention of the birchbark canoe, and the birchbark canoe leaves next to no evidence in the archeological record. Archeological excavations have, however, uncovered worked incisor teeth of the beaver, perhaps used as a blade in a prehistoric crooked knife, a canoe-making tool.

The birchbark canoe was probably highly evolved technically when the Europeans arrived, judging in part by the praise the canoes garnered from the European explorers. Samuel de Champlain was impressed by the birchbark canoes — probably Algonquin — that he saw near Quebec City in 1603. Champlain was mostly responsible for the adoption of the birchbark canoe by the European newcomers. He quickly saw the potential value of these craft to commerce and exploration.

In the seventeenth century, the French lengthened the Native

Hudson's Bay Company canoe, western Quebec, c. 1900. Louis Christopherson, the Hudson's Bay Company post manager at Grand Lake Victoria from 1885 to 1908, is the first white (facing starboard) toward the bow. The long beard of the priest behind him was typical of the Oblate missionaries of western Quebec at the turn of the century and afterwards.

canoes from about twenty feet to thirty-six feet. At the time, the French authorities in what is now Quebec issued licences for trade. Under these licences, the number of canoes was limited. Longer canoes allowed more goods to be carried by the same number of canoes.

The birchbark canoe became the backbone of the French fur trade, and was to take some explorers as far as the Pacific and Arctic oceans. Virtually all of the seventeenth- and eighteenth-century explorers of Canada travelled by birchbark canoe.

The fur trade canoes were, for some, the most memorable birchbark canoe. The French had a birchbark canoe factory at Trois-Rivières, Quebec. The Algonquin of western Quebec and the lower Ottawa River may have been the principal Native group involved in canoe manufacture for the French. To maintain the great store of bark needed by the birchbark canoe factory at Trois-Rivières, there was an extensive trade in rolls of birchbark. Even after 1820, when the Trois-

A fur trade canoe brigade near Grand Lake Victoria in 1885. Louis Christopherson, with his hands crossed, is in the white shirt and flat cap.

Rivières factory was closed, and into this century, birchbark rolls were traded.

One day when I was in Ottawa, I went to the public archives and was able to locate, in the Hudson's Bay Company archives, the journals of the post at Grand Lake Victoria, about 120 miles north of Maniwaki. Louis Christopherson was the Hudson's Bay Company post manager there from 1885 to 1908, and a clerk prior to that. His job included organizing the building of fur trade canoes, on which most of the work was done by Indians hired for the purpose.

As I sat there in the reading room trying to decipher the old script, the post came to life for me. I could imagine the large fur trade canoes coming and going, the two-man canoes leaving for a shorter trip upriver to the post at Lake Barrière, also Christopherson's responsibility.

This birchbark canoe, thought to have been the longest in existence, was last owned by the Buffalo Canoe Club on Lake Erie but was destroyed by fire a few years ago. Believed to have been made by the Algonquin of the lower Ottawa River area around 1860, this canoe weighed 220 pounds. It was 24 feet 9 inches long, had an outer beam of 52.5 inches, an inner beam of 48.5 inches and a depth of 19.5 inches. A single sheet of bark was used to form the bottom of the canoe. The building frame used in its construction was 30 to 32 inches wide at the centre thwart. The stem-piece was wrapped with cedar bark; the lettering was done with natural dyes.

The birchbark canoe remained an important mode of transportation even after the railroad spanned Canada in the late nineteenth century, and in western Quebec it remained so well into the twentieth century. Even at that late date, the birchbark canoe was used by Indians and whites and for trade to and from Hudson's Bay Company posts as far north as James Bay.

My research into birchbark canoes led me to a book from the Smithsonian Institution on the subject. The author's life was as fascinating as his book: Edwin Tappan Adney knew more about the Indians of eastern North America than anyone. He believed that the technical evolution of the birchbark canoe was a long one.

Tappan Adney – he was most often called by his middle name – was born in Athens, Ohio, in 1868. His father, H.H. Adney, was a professor of natural history at Ohio University and had served as acting commander of the 36th Ohio Regiment during the Civil War. In search of other teaching posts, Professor Adney later moved his family to Pennsylvania and North Carolina.

Adney's mother took him and his sister to New York City where she opened a boarding house. Minnie Bell Sharpe, Adney's future wife, came to New York from New Brunswick to study music and met him when she was a guest at the boarding house.

In New York, Adney worked in a lawyer's office by day and in the evenings studied art for three years at the Art Students' League. He would often get up at dawn to study the birds, one of his early passions, in Central Park. He spent much of his time in museums in New York and met Ernest Thompson Seton and other naturalists, who influenced him greatly.

In 1887, at the age of nineteen, he went on what was supposed to be a short visit to New Brunswick, but he ended up staying a year. It was then that he first encountered the Malecites, whose culture he was to study so intently. In Woodstock, he met Peter Jo, a Malecite canoe builder who was about to start building a birchbark canoe. Adney visited Peter Jo's temporary canoe building camp every day to watch him and then made arrangements to come back two years later to build a canoe with him.

In 1889, when Adney returned to Woodstock, he and Peter Jo each built a birchbark canoe. Adney recorded the construction in detailed notes and drawings, and published articles in *Harper's Young People* in 1890, and in *Outing* magazine in May 1900.

Adney went to the Klondike in 1897 to report on the gold rush. Out of his experiences there came a book, *Klondike Stampede*, published in 1900, and articles in *Harper's Weekly* and *The London Chronicle*. He spoke on the Klondike for a New York lecture bureau and lectured also for the Society for the Prevention of Cruelty to Animals.

He was married in 1899, but the following year he returned to the Klondike, this time for *Collier's*. During his time in New York, he also did commercial art and articles and drawings of the outdoors. He made pen-and-ink drawings for *Chapman's Handbook of Birds of Eastern North America*, and illustrated Theodore Roosevelt's book, *Good Hunting*, published in 1907, which the outdoors-minded president inscribed to him.

In 1907, Adney's wife persuaded him to move to New Brunswick where he tried, unsuccessfully, to carry on his father-in-law's nursery business. He began researching heraldry and did some custom bookbinding.

In the next few years, he moved to Montreal and in 1916 entered the Canadian army as a lieutenant of engineers. As well as his other work, he made training models for the Royal Military College.

After the First World War, Adney lived in Montreal and worked as a commercial artist, all the while continuing his other interests — Indians, their birchbark canoes, and heraldry, among other subjects. By the 1920s, his birchbark canoe research was well advanced. His notes were extensive, and he corresponded with people and journeyed to expand the notes. He began what was to be a long correspondence with two well-known directors of the Victoria Museum, later renamed the National Museum of Man: Edward Sapir, subsequently one of North America's best-known linguists, and Diamond Jenness, arguably the most respected anthropologist in Canada.

Old-style Algonquin birchbark canoe from the Ottawa River area in the collection of the National Museum of Denmark. It was made in 1861. The sheer is virtually flat until an abrupt upswing just inboard of the bows. The lower part of the bow is more rounded than would usually be the case. The final three gores, closest to the bows, help raise the bark for the greater height required for this peak.

To Sapir, Adney wrote in 1925 that he was doing window advertising for the T. Eaton Company in Montreal. Knowing of Adney's work with birchbark canoes, Sapir replied that he hoped Adney's book would soon be finished so that the Victoria Museum could have the privilege of publishing it. The same year Adney reported that he was working on the canoe book to the exclusion of his regular work.

Adney also told Sapir at that time that the Hudson's Bay Company had referred him to two men who had experience with the old fur trade canoes. One of the men lived in La Sarre, Quebec, and the other in North Bay, Ontario. The man in North Bay was Louis Christopherson, the former Hudson's Bay Company factor at Grand Lake Victoria in western Quebec. He had supervised Indians in the building of a great number of freighter canoes. It is largely upon his information that the fur trade chapter in Adney's *Bark Canoes and Skin Boats of North America* is based. Christopherson died in North Bay in 1928.

No fur trade canoes remain now, though they were common and still being made at the turn of this century. None of these long canoes were preserved, mostly because people thought they were so common that they did not need to be collected.

Hunters' canoes from Maniwaki and Rapid Lake, however, are seen frequently in museums. Although these canoes generally are well made, some people deprecate them because they're more common than other birchbark canoes. Hunters' canoes should be viewed in the context of their importance to the continent. Five hundred years from now, the few score of preserved birchbark canoes from western Quebec will be priceless.

On one occasion in 1925, Adney asked Sapir if he could arrange a pass for him on Canadian National Railways to travel for research. Adney's funds were low, a condition that seemed to plague him throughout his life. Sapir was unable to help.

Adney wrote to Diamond Jenness over a period of fifteen years. As early as 1926, Jenness discussed with Adney publishing specifics about his birchbark canoe work — whether they would do colour plates, for example. He often invited Adney to visit him at the Victoria Museum, which he did on occasion. Eventually Adney gave Diamond Jenness and Marius Barbeau (the Canadian ethnographer and scholar who published more than a hundred books on traditional North American cultures) most of the credit for encouraging him to continue his research into Aboriginal canoes.

Adney told Jenness of his efforts to get more information on Aboriginal canoes — for example, an Iroquois elm bark canoe from Grand River Reserve, which he was comparing at the time with St. Francis River Abnaki and Malecite elm bark canoes. He also spoke to Jenness of a spruce bark canoe from British Columbia, bark canoes from Churchill, and Athabasca and Yukon Aboriginal canoes, which he believed to be Inuit in origin. He thought that Aboriginal canoes emerged *de novo* in separate regions.

Adney looked for canoe origins not in birch areas but in areas of elm, spruce, and similar trees found beyond the limits of birch growth. The bark of these trees could not be cut and sewn like birchbark; the sheet had to be dealt with whole. He classed canoes according to the way the builder solved the problem of making the bottom both level and wide enough for travel in streams of shallow depth. This problem was solved in one way in the canoes of the eastern woodlands, in another way in the Athabascan canoes, and in yet another manner in the western canoes with their pointed ends. Among western canoes, Adney included not only those of the Kootenays of British Columbia but also those of the Amur of Siberia.

He spoke to Indians, took photos, and made sketches. He also began to make one-fifth scale models of Aboriginal canoes, including some from Japan and Siberia, as well as models of hide boats and canoes of bark other than birchbark. By 1930, the model collection numbered more than ninety, and he valued it at twenty-five thousand dollars. The collection eventually contained more than one hundred models.

Occasionally Adney tried to make a little money in trading. For forty dollars he offered Jenness an eight-foot-eight-inch Tête-de-Boule hunting canoe that he had purchased at Manouan, Quebec. He was prepared to sell another fourteen-foot canoe for fifty dollars. At the time, the going price of Indian-built birchbark canoes was about one dollar a foot. The smaller of these two canoes eventually ended up in the collection of the ethnographical museum in Göteborg, Sweden.

By 1929, Minnie Adney was blind, and so in the early 1930s the Adneys returned to Upper Woodstock, New Brunswick, where Minnie died in 1937. Adney wrote to Jenness informing him that Minnie had died, and also that Adney had gone broke in Montreal a few years

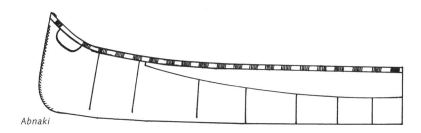

Abnaki

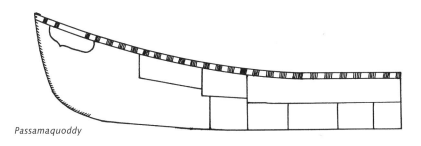

Ojibway long-nose

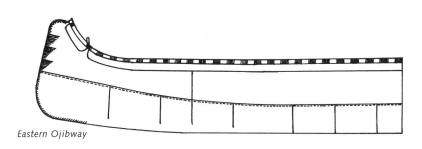

Eastern Ojibway

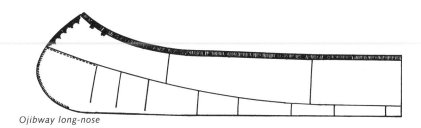

Passamaquoddy

Profiles of Native canoes

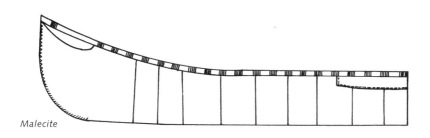

Malecite

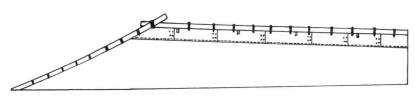

Beothuk

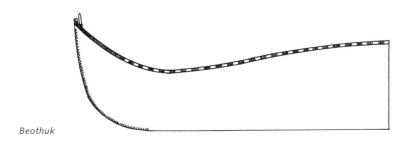

Kootenay

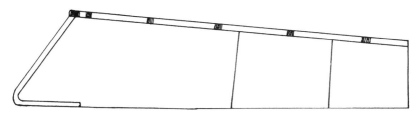

Tungus (Siberian)

Edwin Tappan Adney's "bungalow," as he called it, at Upper Woodstock, New Brunswick. Here he worked on his drawings, notes and canoe models.

before. Along with his wife's declining health, Adney's financial situation was the reason they moved back to New Brunswick.

Adney's notes and research might have been lost to ethnographers and would probably never have been published had it not been for Mr. and Mrs. Frederick Hill. Hill was the director of the Mariners' Museum in Newport News, Virginia. Although the museum's collection included a great representation of nautical vessels and paraphernalia from around the world, the collection contained almost no North American Aboriginal watercraft. Mrs. Hill travelled with her husband to collect materials for the museum. Her manuscript, "The Museum Pieces," describes how they found Adney.

On a visit to Montreal in 1940, they saw Adney's model collection at the ethnological museum at McGill University. The models had been stacked carelessly and a note nearby said "On loan from E. Tappan Adney." The Hills were impressed with the collection, but struck by the lack of credit Adney was accorded. They wanted to find out more about the man and his impressive collection. All they could learn at the time was that the collection had been left as collateral for a loan. The museum did not have Adney's address, but the Hills finally learned that Adney was living in New Brunswick, so they travelled there to meet him.

They found Adney on the outskirts of Woodstock, living in what remained of a decrepit barn, called by him and others his bungalow. The bungalow's fireplace, constructed of heavy fieldstone, took up most of one wall; he did some cooking on this fireplace. There was also a window ten feet long that faced the St. John River. The place was furnished with homemade furniture and there was no plumbing. Canoe models were everywhere. One small room of the bungalow was packed with birchbark, willow, ash, and spruce root for canoe models.

Adney appreciated the Hills' interest in his work, an interest that contrasted with the lack of appreciation he had experienced in Montreal and elsewhere. They could see that he needed money. He regretted that his valuable model canoe collection was still in Montreal and that the museum there had shown no interest in acquiring it permanently. The Hills informed Adney that the Mariners' Museum would be interested in purchasing the model collection.

During the Hills' visit and in later correspondence, Adney told them of the project of his lifetime — a monograph on the bark canoes of North America. By the time they met him, he had already done much of the work. Indeed, some parts, such as the introduction, had already been through several drafts.

His working title was generally "The Bark Canoes of North America." An earlier one had been "The Bark Canoes of North America with notes on other bark canoe areas — Northeastern Asia, Australia,

South America, Europe." In this earlier manuscript, he developed theories, later left out of the published book, on the migrations of the prehistoric peoples in northern North America, as illustrated by their canoes. He made qualitative judgements about canoes: "The birchbark canoe had begun to deteriorate in workmanship almost from the time when nails began to be used in place of the wooden pegs." Adney took notes on canoes from the Jesuit Relations, annual reports prepared and sent to Paris by the Canadian mission of the Society of Jesus, and from the writings of Alexander Henry, Alexander Mackenzie, Alexander Ross, Louis-Joseph Gaultier de La Vérendrye, David Thompson, and other fur traders and explorers. He also delved extensively into the Montreal archives for information on fur trade canoes. He tried to read documents in the original French, as he reasoned that translators might not be familiar with watercraft.

In the early 1940s when the Hills were getting to know Adney, his notes were particularly chaotic and only partially written up into a general description of his work from the late 1920s on. The Mariners' Museum worked out an agreement with Adney: the museum would pay off his loan of one thousand dollars from the Montreal museum, give him an additional payment for the model collection, and pay him a monthly stipend to allow him to complete his canoe book. He continued to work at his crudely built table in the bungalow outside of Woodstock.

The Hills regretted that they were taking the valuable model collection out of the country "where it rightfully belonged," but perhaps their consciences were assuaged by the fact that responsible people in Canada seemed to take so little interest in it.

From 1940 when they first met him, the Hills visited Adney in New Brunswick once or twice a year. They were extremely solicitous of his welfare and bought him canned goods, clothes, and a typewriter. They also had electricity installed in his bungalow, and told Adney to send

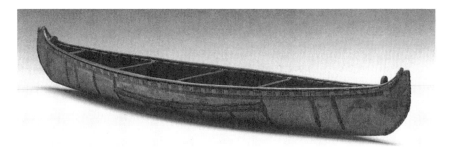

Model of old-style Algonquin birchbark canoe made about 1920 by Ottawa River Algonquin at the reserve at Golden Lake, Ontario. The pictures of animals hunted by the Indians were added to the model in 1927 by Lamab Sarazin.

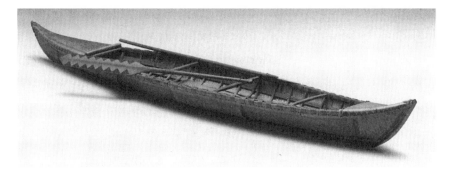

Model of a Malecite River birchbark canoe. It is typical of Saint John River canoes of 1880 to 1890. The decoration, spirals and women's earring patterns, were scraped into the winter bark.

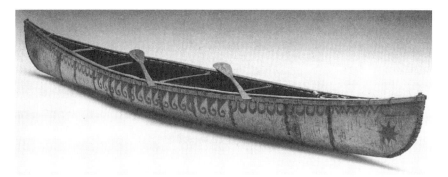

Athabaskan birchbark kayak of the Dogrib Chippewa.

them a bill for repairing his roof. This bill is still in the files of the Mariners' Museum.

On the rare occasions when Adney was a few dollars ahead, he spent the surplus on his Indian friends. As the years went on, he seemed more easily diverted from "The Bark Canoes of North America." More and more he spent time championing the Indians' cause against the federal and local governments — to the detriment of the canoe book and to the frustration of the Mariners' Museum.

Peter Paul, his Malecite friend, said that Adney would have made a poor attorney because of his temper. Perhaps because of his work as a young man in a New York lawyer's office, Adney thought otherwise.

Peter Paul was arrested for cutting ash on private land without permission. When Adney heard this, he determined to go to court with Paul to fight the charge. Paul began to see that Adney, because of his temper, was not much of an asset. Adney wouldn't allow the farmer to finish what he was saying, and after three interruptions, the judge asked Adney to leave the court house.

Around this time, Adney even began a book on Indian difficulties with the government. He was becoming restless and irritable. His son said his father did not have the discipline necessary for recognition in any one field. Another of Adney's worries was that his work on bark canoes would not be published as he intended. He had before shown himself to be sensitive to an editor's tampering with his work.

When the 125 canoe models were sent from Montreal to the Mariners' Museum, Adney was invited to Virginia to add to the museum's information on them. The Hills met him at Grand Central Station in New York City for the ride down to Virginia. He created quite an impression. He was lean and over six feet tall, with erect posture and close-cropped hair. A newspaperman who interviewed him about this time described him as having "dark and restless eyes."

When he met the Hills at the train station, he was wearing a coonskin cap a few sizes too small. From the cap, a long tail dangled around his neck. The front of his coat was green and stained. His overshoes were unfastened and flopped on the station floor. He was happy and excited to be meeting the Hills in New York, and his mood and appearance helped to make him the centre of attention in the station.

Adney told the Hills that Indians should be encouraged to return to their ancestral ways – living in bark shelters, cooking outside at least for the summer months, and continuing to make their traditional crafts. Such a return, he believed, would help them physically and emotionally and restore their self-respect.

He felt that the Indians had taught the white man all he knows about wildlife. He claimed that the only European settlements that survived in Florida were the ones whose inhabitants made friends with the Indians and learned the cultivation of corn. And how far, Adney asked, would the white man have penetrated in North America without the birchbark canoe and the web snowshoe?

He wrote to Diamond Jenness about the moving of the model collection to the Mariners' Museum in Virginia. His long-time correspondent responded, "I am sorry your model canoe collection had to go outside Canada, but after all, we want to abolish that boundary line between ourselves and our neighbors as much as we can."

Canadian nationalists today would cringe at that statement, but such treatment as Adney received is repeated even nowadays and, coincidentally, in the same field.

In 1979, a friend of mine who was an ethnologist on the staff of the National Museum of Man was going up to Hudson Bay to document the canoe-building process of a rather remarkable Cree master builder, one of the few living. The ethnologist was obliged to use only a thirty-five-millimetre camera. The museum had a staff film photographer, but during that time the photographer was required to stay in Ottawa to film the director's golf tournament!

Adney became weaker as he entered his eighties. But he could count on the Indians. An Indian man and his wife came to his bungalow regularly to clean, do his laundry, and cook for him.

He died on October 10, 1950. The bungalow in Upper Woodstock was filled from top to bottom with canoe models, paddles, salmon spears, toboggans, arrowheads, knives, axes, and stone relics. His son gave all Adney's notes and papers to the Mariners' Museum. The Mariners' Museum decided that Adney's notes on linguistics were outside its scope and gave them to the Peabody Museum in Salem, Massachusetts.

Since the canoe papers were still not in publishable form, the Mariners' Museum hired Howard I. Chapelle, curator of transportation at the Smithsonian Institution, to revise them. Chapelle worked on them intermittently during the mid-1950s, but the Adney manuscript, as written up and organized by Chapelle, was shelved when it was completed.

Chapelle's revision of Adney's manuscript was eventually published by the Smithsonian Institution in 1964 as *The Bark Canoes and Skin Boats of North America*, by Edwin Tappan Adney and Howard I. Chapelle (Bulletin No. 230). Adney's passion, a love of the Indians and a fascination with their watercraft, which had held him – and sometimes impoverished him – since 1887, had reached its culmination.

The book is an enduring memorial to Edwin Tappan Adney, and is still in print and available at the Smithsonian Institution. One can sometimes point to a book as being the best in its field. *The Bark Canoes and Skin Boats of North America* is virtually the only one in its field.

It diverges in a number of ways from Adney's original plan. He had intended to have his scale models play a large part in the book. The title was to have been *The Bark Canoes of North America*, although according to notes Adney left, he would probably have included some material on the skin boats of the Woodland and Plains Indians. Adney also had information on transitional canoes – canvas canoes built in the birchbark canoe style – of the Cree. Material on the kayak and umiak was added by Chapelle because he had done some work of his own on the subject.

Adney's preface to his book, written in 1941, reveals his admiration for Indian canoe makers:

> We shall pursue as far as possible the policy of mentioning the various Indian craftsmen who have supplied us with direct knowledge on details of canoe construction and decoration. These men have earned the right to personal recognition as much if not more so than artists who sign their names to unsold canvasses, or are legitimately entitled to be known before the public by name.

In *The Bark Canoes and Skin Boats of North America*, birchbark canoes are discussed according to the different Native groups that made them. When reading a section entitled "Tête-de-Boule," I was struck by something strange: the only two places named as Tête-de-Boule settlements are Barrière and Grand Lake Victoria. I had always thought of these as Algonquin settlements. Then I looked at the canoes. They seemed to be on the northern Algonquin model of the *wâbanäki tcîmân* and not the type of canoe I had seen from Tête-de-Boule (Attikamek) reserves to the east, such as Manouan. I did some research and found that ethnologists, linguists, the Department of Indian Affairs, and the Indians themselves regard both these places as Algonquin. While divisions between Native groups, particularly in the Algonquian family, are difficult to determine and there is much overlap, it seemed odd that there were about twenty sources saying these people were Algonquin and either Adney or Chapelle saying they were not.

Adney says the Algonquin themselves may have been the first to build birchbark canoes for the French. He adds that one of their canoe models, called the old-style or *rabeska*, may have been the model for the large fur trade canoes.

The old-style Algonquin canoe had a straight sheer — the top line of the canoe — that rose sharply near the end. The rocker, or bottom line, was also rather straight and curved gently at the end to follow the stem-piece, which became nearly vertical and then tumbled home slightly.

Then, perhaps at the end of the nineteenth century, the Algonquin of western Quebec started building another model they called *wâbanäki tcîmân*. In Algonquin, the literal meaning of the term is "Abnaki canoe." It appears that the Abnaki Indians, who were located on the St. Francis River east of Montreal in the late 1800s, were selling their canoes to white sportsmen. The Abnaki canoes were brought into the Algonquin territory by the Hudson's Bay Company. They would have come through Montreal and then up the Ottawa River to the post at Mattawa.

The fact that many sportsmen were using these Abnaki canoes may have been one of the influences that caused the Algonquin to copy the Abnaki model. The Algonquin then evolved slightly different methods of building on the Abnaki model, so that their canoes could still be differentiated from the Abnaki canoes. Adney says that the Algonquin, in turn, influenced the Abnaki practices.

Around the turn of the century, the factor at Mattawa was Colin Rankin. His Hudson's Bay Company post served several of the more distant Algonquin posts, as well as Cree posts as far away as James Bay, five hundred miles to the north.

In 1904, Rankin wrote to a man in Massachusetts that "the trip from Mattawa to James Bay can be made with two or three men paddling and the canoe not too heavily laden in three weeks; if more men employed the trip can be made in a few days less time."

Fort William, Quebec, a Hudson's Bay Company post in the mid-nineteenth century. Ernestine Gidmark holds a fur trade canoe building frame from that era.

In response to an inquiry for a job at one of the posts from a man in England, Rankin replied that he could not give much in wages for a year or two until the man could learn to keep accounts and speak Indian.

Adney took note of articles that mentioned the canoes in Mattawa. Two were written by Julian Ralph and appeared in *Harper's* magazine in 1890 and 1892. Ralph wrote about the post at Mattawa that "an outbuilding in the rear of the trading storehouse is the repository of scores of birchbark canoes – the carriages of British North America."

Adney noted that Ralph had seen Mattawa only in the winter, but if he had come in summer, "he might still have seen *grands canots* coming in from the posts in the near north, gaily painted as of yore, with paddles tipped in blue, if he had encountered the brigade of Mr. Christopherson, for instance, bringing in the winter's catch of furs from Grand Lake Victoria in western Québec."

CHAPTER 4

For all that I was learning about the history of the birchbark canoe, I was not making much practical progress. I had made a small birchbark canoe, three feet long and rather crude, with a young Indian boy who lived at the other end of the reserve, but that was the sum of my accomplishment.

While my attempts to learn birchbark canoe construction were stymied, my study of the Algonquin language was overwhelming. There were so many things to learn, and what I did learn was so filled with splendour. I made a list of five words to learn per day, and I practised continually with Mrs. Carle.

There are fascinating expressions in the language and intriguing customs that are reflected in it. Some of these I gleaned from Abbot Cuoq's lexicon, from compilations of words that in some cases had been made a few centuries before. Many of the things described have disappeared and are no longer familiar to living Algonquin.

During my studies I discovered a word I was sure I could use when describing what it was like to make a living as a writer. *Nikikwâtis* means living as an otter, which in turn means that some poor soul is without means; he has only his canoe and his paddle.

Otagwänipîsan is the word for rainbow and the literal meaning is "coat that the rain wears." There is an aphrodisiac called *akoskowewack*. Then there is the very evocative *ajawisikanendamawacin*, a mark of affection, which means "pour it (a liquid) from your mouth into mine" and refers to a practice that only the old remember. *Memegwesiwak* are playful little spirits that inhabit the depths of lakes. Then there is the interesting euphemism, *agwätcing potawe*, "she is making her fire outside," said many years ago about a woman who was menstruating and, during that time, was obliged to make her fire outside and stay in a small lodge.

Kiwekîjik and *kiwepipôn* mean respectively the day is going back (where it came from), and winter is going back (where it came from) – end of day and end of winter. How little poetry some of our Indo-European languages seem to have when compared to Algonquin.

Some of the missionary linguists, Cuoq especially, used Latin to define Algonquin words having to do with sex, as in, for example, *kaiatase: puella, virgo* (virgin). Or sometimes the missionaries wrote phrases in Latin simply because they were used to doing so. Although I had a Latin dictionary in the cabin, a few years of goofing off in Latin class in my Catholic high school came back to haunt me, and I was often nonplussed. If the reader is neither an Algonquin nor a Latinist, he is left in the dark when reading the works of these missionaries.

During the long winter nights, when it started to get dark at four o'clock, I made big pots of tea and pored over the Cuoq lexicon for the fascinating insights it gave into the Algonquin culture. Sometimes my studies made me forget to have supper.

Abwisak is the word for paddle wood, that is, maple, because ordinarily maple was used for paddles. The earth is *akamik*, because long ago people noticed that the beaver took material from the bottom of the lake; they thought all of the earth that was out of water was the work of the beaver. *Anoki* means to work, but the term is employed most often in the sense of hunting, because hunting is the usual work of Indians.

Kitabiki means to get out of a steel trap. It is said figuratively of one who succeeds in paying off his debts. *Kitcikanakwat* is a verb signifying a sky dappled with clouds, to the Algonquin a sign of snow. *Mananjite* means to cut cedar branches to sleep upon. *Manataam* has a combined meaning — to sing badly or to paddle badly, or both, because canoeists in Canada were in the habit of singing as they paddled.

Folklore is naturally much a part of the language. *Michilimakina-gok* is a kind of sorcerer who lives in the woods, heard by many but never seen by anyone.

The translation of some words is curious. The real meaning of raspberry, *miskwimin*, is "blood berry," because they resemble conglomerated drops of blood. Some practical definitions point to something I could try one day: *namakwan* is a kind of pomade used to protect the body from bites by mosquitoes and no-see-ums; turtle fat was good, Cuoq recorded. ·

Okaninabob is a bouillon made of bones. When the Algonquin were short of provisions, they'd break open bones and put them in the soup.

Watap is, of course, spruce root, and that's Cuoq's first definition, but he added a figurative definition as well, an intriguing one. The word could also mean muscles and tendons: if a person was extremely thin, it was said that he was no more than frame and *watap*.

There is a cliché that the Inuit have fifteen words for snow. An amazing number of Algonquin words deal with the canoe; I found nearly two hundred. Some of these words came from the Lemoine and Cuoq dictionaries and some from a fine dictionary compiled recently by Ernest McGregor, former chief of the River Désert Algonquin in Maniwaki. But the preponderance came from the Indian birchbark canoe builders I knew.

Most words were alike in the Algonquin of Maniwaki and Rapid

Lake, though there were occasional differences. For the most part, the specialized vocabulary of birchbark canoe building was known only to the canoe builders; other people in the community tended to be unfamiliar with it.

There is one word for fishing from a canoe and another for just fishing. There is the old word, *apickamon,* for a piece of bark put under one's knees to cushion them while one is paddling.

Sometimes I got a practical tip just by reading the dictionary. According to Cuoq, the word *apikotazowin* means a piece of cloth put in the hand to avoid blisters while carving with the crooked knife. I tried using such a piece of cloth, and it was a fine improvement.

The reason bark is most often rejected for a canoe is that it is brittle or dry. The Algonquin have a word for it — *kapackweia.*

There is the curious word *piwikotagan* that means shavings from a crooked knife, as differentiated from shavings from another knife or a hand plane. This word is an indication of how discriminating the language is.

I remember that Jim Jerome, an Algonquin canoe builder, told me about the *pokogan,* a shelter made of saplings and covered with birchbark that is constructed over the canoe building bed. I had never seen one, but Jim had constructed them.

◆

There was also plenty to learn about Indian languages in general. At one time, there were more than two hundred Indian languages in North America, but a number of them have disappeared. Most of the languages were as different from each other as German is from Swahili. Recently, a linguistic census of the more than a score of Indian groups in California found that nearly all the languages of these groups had only up to three speakers. A U.S. senator from California made a name for himself not long ago by being a proponent of English-only laws.

Native American languages are, it seems, at the bottom of the demographic/linguistic scale.

The Algonquin language is in the Algonquian linguistic family, the widest-ranging family geographically. Reaching from the Naskapi and Montagnais people in Labrador and eastern Quebec all the way to the Blackfoot and Cheyenne in western Canada and the western United States, Algonquian languages were even spoken in several small communities in the California mountains. The Algonquin in the Maniwaki area could actually communicate quite well with the Ojibway as far west as Minnesota and Manitoba. As I was to learn later, in fact, these languages are actually rather close, with just a few differences in vocabulary. The Algonquin language, however, has virtually nothing in common with the Iroquois language used only 150 miles to the south. Perhaps only a handful of words are similar in these languages.

Algonquin is a systematic, highly complex language, and one that has continued to develop. At first I was puzzled by the existence of words for things like trains that did not exist centuries ago. Then it dawned on me that these words did not exist in English or French years ago, either. The Indians did not take any longer to develop a word to describe a train than the English did. *Ickote otâbân* figuratively means "train" and literally, "fire wagon," which perhaps describes it better than the English word. The same is true of the Indian expressions for rifle, airplane, and automobile – the terms were created as the objects came into use. It is not difficult to invent words for new objects and concepts – this is done constantly in the Indo-European languages.

As I studied, I learned that there are thirteen cases of nouns in Algonquin. Verbs can be conjugated in nine modes and seven tenses and are the key part of speech. To indicate the colour black, for example, one does not use the adjective for black. Instead, one has to conjugate the verb that means *be* black. Once I took out the synoptic table of verbs and counted the letters in one of the long suffixes that is added to a verb. Each of the letters or verbal particles of one, two, or three letters has a grammatical importance. One of the suffixes has nineteen letters.

There are other grammatical calisthenics to work out. *Ni wâbäma* means "I see him"; to say "he sees me," the pronoun remains the same, but the verb ending changes and becomes *ni wâbämik*. This lone example may not appear difficult, but all persons and tenses have similar surprises, so that the body of the grammar constitutes something rather unfathomable.

Mrs. Carle told me something I was to hear many times. Given the fact that, thanks to the French missionaries, the Algonquin language has a long written history — more than three hundred years — and was obviously deeply respected by them, her story came as a shock. She said that in the reserve school in Maniwaki some years ago, Indian children were punished for speaking their language, even to the point of being slapped if they spoke it. I later heard the same story from many other areas. The Tahitians and the Irish are other peoples who have experienced this sort of linguistic oppression by colonialists.

What's more, although French was the predominant language in Maniwaki, the village that abuts the reserve, the federal government chose to give Algonquin children school instruction in English. Their native language was without a place in the curriculum, and the government deemed French unsuitable to take the place of Algonquin.

An anthropologist put this language issue in another context for me later. He visited Maniwaki from a large university in the United States, and we discussed the reserve school's language situation, which had seemed to me to be an attack not only on the Algonquin language but also on French. Although I had no training in anthropology, I appreciated his perspective. He said that instructing the local Indian population in the English language may have preserved Indian culture. His theory was that teaching English to the Algonquin in a French-speaking region served to separate them from the local French people, and thus to stave off assimilation and help to preserve Indian culture. He never mentioned whether his theory might have application throughout the rest of North America. I wondered, for example, if teaching French to Indian communities outside of Quebec, say in Arizona, would lead to their using it as their primary language.

◆

Mrs. Carle was endlessly helpful with the language. She mentioned one day that, in Algonquin, May is *wâbikon kîzis*, which means "month of the flowers." Her comment sent me off on another tangent, following the trail of the poetic significations of the Indian language.

The months of summer, I found, have names of berries. June, July, and August are named after the strawberry, raspberry, and blackberry. October and November are named after the trout and whitefish, each spawning in the month named after it. From time to time in my reading, I saw the names of the months in other Indian languages. These words are invariably different from those used in Algonquin, and so provide one more indication of the pluralism of Indian culture.

The Algonquin language held many wonders for me and presented many challenges. It did not distract me, though, from my original desire to build a birchbark canoe.

CHAPTER 5

On a warm day in May 1977, while I was contentedly walking home from the post office with a smile on my face, I passed by William's shop on my way.

In retrospect, I realize this meeting opened the door to my future in canoe building. "Did you win the lottery or something?" he asked. He was always a good conversationalist and a good listener.

"Better than that," I told him. Into every diligent writer's life a little sunshine will eventually come. I was returning from the post office with the initial shipment of my first published book, which had recently come from the presses. Even most new fathers don't experience such delight. The book would not make much of a splash, but I felt that the door was open and the sky was the limit.

"I just had a book published," I replied.

"Oh?" He seemed interested.

I opened the box and took out a book. William looked at it closely.

"Can I keep this?" he asked. His first language was Algonquin, but he read in French and English whenever he could.

"Sure, go ahead," I said. I suspected he was going to read my book to see if there really was anything about Indians in it, although I told him that there was not. One can't be too careful with white men.

I had little contact with William that summer. I was writing and travelling around the country to promote the book that had just come out. I assumed William's refusal to teach a white man to build a birchbark canoe was final. Nor did I try to make a full-size birchbark canoe on my own. The most I did was to stop by his shop occasionally and view a birchbark canoe under construction. It was a fairly active time for him; he was making three or four canoes per season, helped by his wife, Mary, and by some grandchildren to whom he was trying to teach the craft.

In the fall of that year, I had a chance to do something I had always wanted to do – stay by myself for a period of time far out in the woods. An Indian trapper was going to lend me his cabin forty miles west of Maniwaki, and I was preparing supplies for the stay. The greatest joy was gathering up my writing supplies and a large number of books.

More than books or typing supplies, however, I needed a little survival knowledge. I asked one of the old-timers, Hans Andersen, to help me out. If he was related to the famous Danish writer it would only be distantly. Hans had come over from Denmark with his parents when he was twelve, and they settled on a homestead near Maniwaki. What was unique about Hans was not that he had spent all his life in the wilderness, but that he actually loved the woods and the winter of Quebec. He was in his late seventies when I met him, and even then he worked all alone, deep in the woods, as caretaker for some isolated hunting and fishing camps.

Hans was a fine-looking man with a smile ready for everyone. When he smiled, his eyes lit up in a way that suggested, if you were telling a story, that he suspected you of lacing it with a little hyperbole, or, if he were telling the story, that he might be doing the same thing.

Hans and I often met on the main street of Maniwaki as he passed for his daily (or sometimes twice-daily) coffee break at the local hotel. With his jauntily cocked hat and his sprightly gait, he couldn't be mistaken for anyone else. Often as not, a few casual words of greeting would evolve into an all-day conversation. His talk was almost always of the woods.

Although he had completed only a few years of grade school, Hans was a literate fellow who read a lot and was very articulate. He spoke Danish, French, and English, and had a passable ability in Indian. He was a bushman, but not a hermit.

We spent a lot of time talking in the kitchen of his house on the edge of town, chatting over gallons of coffee and Hans's special stew, which he made — or perhaps it would be more accurate to say warmed up — almost every midday. From a butcher he bought a package of chicken giblets at the reasonable price of sixteen cents a pound and made a stew out of them that lasted for a longer time than good-tasting food would be expected to last. Each noon he warmed up his stew and served it over potatoes.

Unlike many others I spoke to about my intended sojourn, Hans gave me all manner of advice and encouragement. The latter was perhaps the more important. Many worried about my safety, but others voiced another concern: how much would it pay? They thought me crazy when they found out that the experience would pay nothing and would be abstemious in the extreme. Why would anyone want to go into the woods for a winter when there were any number of jobs in the city where a person could make good money?

But Hans was full of encouragement: he thought my coming adventure was a great thing to do and got fired up just talking about it. So in his kitchen, my plans evolved over coffee and chicken-giblet stew. Hans offered me every material aid but his kitchen sink. To help ward off the cold, he gave me a heavy winter shirt and wool socks. He loaned me a type of packsack that is rarely seen anymore. Mostly it looked like an ordinary sack — shoulder straps attached to a heavy canvas bag — but at the top a tumpline was affixed. He also offered me a good supply of food, mostly canned goods, but also sacks of navy beans.

More important were the tips Hans gave me: wear two or three pairs of socks if it is very cold. Never get sweaty when you're walking or you'll freeze. He told me to bring a good supply of candles in addition to a lantern, because candles are cheaper and easier to use. Always make sure that the lantern is out at night; never set the candle in such a way that it could fall over. Make sure that all the openings in the walls of the cabin are chinked; even a little one can make quite a difference to the inside temperature. Watch the potatoes and onions so they don't freeze; if they freeze more than once, they'll be no good. Wrap them in a coat if necessary. Get a pair of one-piece woollen underwear. Before going into the woods, accumulate old newspapers; they're fine for starting a fire and are good for putting into a coat when you're walking into a cold headwind.

I asked Hans about animals, edible and dangerous. As far as he was concerned, there were no dangerous animals in the woods, except perhaps a she-bear with cubs or a bull moose during the rutting season. As for wolves, he did not fear them, never having had an untoward encounter with one. When he was a young man, wolves had once followed him so closely in the woods that he could hear their panting, though he could not see them. He had never heard of anyone being attacked by wolves, but they were known to follow people at times.

Hans said that if he had his choice between beaver and any other kind of meat, he would take beaver, and he advised me to get some if I could.

I tried to analyze his diet to figure out what I should have for the woods and maybe for life, as the man was quite healthy and almost eighty. As nearly as I could figure out, the reason for his longevity and health lay in his chicken-gut stew.

His small house in town was only a *pied-à-terre* where he kept a room. During the fall, he rented the rest of the house to a woman who had a number of children. When Hans was in town, they shared the kitchen stove. It did not involve much sharing, as Hans had only to warm up the stew. One evening the woman had the whole kitchen busy with the evening meal for herself and her children. The burners on the stove, including the one where the chicken-gut stew was warming, were all full.

The woman looked at Hans standing over his stew, slowly stirring it as it warmed. "Oh, for God's sake, Hans, take some of our potato salad. You need something a little different."

Hans looked over approvingly at the potato salad on the counter next to the stove. "By God, that does look good. Thank you. I think I will. That's very kind of you." And he took two big ladles full of the potato salad and put them in the stew.

His practical advice was nearly unlimited.

"If you've got an ax or lantern or something, don't leave it in the cabin. They'll steal it on you sure as can be," Hans said.

This worried me a bit. I did not relish hauling my things back to town when I needed to make a trip away from the cabin.

"All you need to do," he said, "is to cache them in the bush. Take your valuable things and put them away from the cabin a ways. And another thing: if you can find a big, hollow cedar log, put them there. Nothing will rust on you."

We paused for a moment, during which he started another pot of coffee.

He went on. "I did that one winter when I was out on the Coulonge River," he said, naming a river about sixty miles west of Maniwaki. "I had a bunch of traps and I didn't want anyone to come along and take them. So I cached them in a hollow cedar log and do you know, when I got back there, not only were the traps still there, they were as dry as a bone. There wasn't a speck of rust on them."

"How long was it before you got back to them?" I asked.

"Oh, I don't know." He thought for a moment. "It must have been twenty-seven or twenty-eight years."

◆

In the midst of all the preparations for my winter in the bush, something quite unexpected happened.

I was walking past William's house one day when he motioned to me to come over to the porch.

"Do you remember that you asked me about a year ago if I would teach you how to make a birchbark canoe?"

It was ancient history. I was not going to lament something that was not going to be.

"If you want to come here and stay with us and help us, I'll teach you to make a birchbark canoe. Mary and I have to go away often to exhibitions, and we would like someone to watch the house. If you want to do that for us, I'll teach you how to make a birchbark canoe and snowshoes."

The invitation was a bolt out of the blue. How could I let the opportunity pass by? I did, but only because it was November — not the time for building birchbark canoes — and I had already spent a lot of time planning for my winter in the woods. I told William where I planned to spend the next few months and asked him if I could come back and see him in the spring.

CHAPTER 6

I was ensconced in the cabin on a little lake forty miles from Maniwaki for a good part of the winter. In addition to trying to write and to survive, I went through the Adney book from time to time and thought about how I would build my own birchbark canoe. Adney had a fair amount of information on the Algonquin canoes.

Occasionally a question recurred: Had William Commanda *really* said that he would teach me how to make a birchbark canoe? I knew I could make a birchbark canoe on my own eventually, and a good one if I stayed at it long enough, but learning from an Indian canoe maker would be so much more rewarding than learning from one of the white men who had learned how to make a birchbark canoe, which, in turn, would have been more interesting than learning from a book.

I went down the list of reasons that might have caused William to change his mind. The only plausible reason for his change of heart was my sincerity in learning the Algonquin language. I had stayed on the reserve for more than a year to study the language. He could see when I spoke to him in Algonquin that I had made progress.

"Yes, you come here and watch the house for us and I will teach you how to make a birchbark canoe," William said on the first opportunity I had to see him in the spring. "As I told you before, Mary and I go away often. We want someone to take care of the house while we're gone."

I fetched my things and moved into the Commanda house.

William and Mary's home was situated at an intersection on the reserve's main highway that ran north into the centre of Maniwaki, about three-fourths of a mile distant, and south to Ottawa eighty miles away. There was a constant rush of traffic, including big transports that, when I was in the midst of a light sleep, seemed as though they were coming through the basement of William's house. The road that connected with the highway near William's house was Bitobi Road. It ran west into the main part of the reserve — mostly wilderness — and many houses were located along it.

The house had two storeys and a porch ran around two sides. Here William would sit on summer evenings and watch the traffic go by. The largest bedroom was on the first floor. The two bedrooms upstairs were not completely separated. I moved into one side of the upstairs room and Mary's brother, Basil Smith, who had been a guide and trapper all his life, had the other side. He had been staying there for many years. When I moved in with the Commandas in 1978, he was sixty-eight, two years older than William. Basil guided in the summer and part of the fall. In late fall and early winter, he trapped with his trapping part- ner, Jocko Carle. When the snow became too deep, he went back to the house and called it a season.

William, Mary, and Basil were the only permanent inhabitants of the house, but grandchildren were almost permanent. The Commandas' daughter and her four children lived next door. Their son and his six children lived across the road.

With the warmth of spring, William and Mary returned to their habit of sitting on the porch after supper, Basil and I joining them.

"Look at those birchbark canoes going by," Mary said more than once when a large transport passed the house, turned the corner, and went toward the veneer plant several hundred yards away. The trucks were loaded with heavy birch logs, some of them two feet in diameter and fifteen feet long – just the size necessary for a birchbark canoe.

William, Mary, and Basil were among the most skillful exponents of trilingualism in Maniwaki. In the course of a day, they spoke French, English, and Algonquin. With each other and with old Indians who came by – and with me, when I wasn't lazy – they spoke their first language, Algonquin. Most of the time with their son and daughter and their spouses and all the time with their grandchildren they spoke English. With French people from town, they spoke French. When William and Mary were speaking to each other, most of the conversation would be in Algonquin, with a few sentences in French, and some in English sprinkled here and there.

My problem with learning Algonquin was quite obvious: dealing with a transitive verb with more than twelve hundred endings was a job for a computer. The temptation to speak to the native speaker in the easiest common language was even greater than if I had been learning a European language.

Basil was a continual help. He was always the best person for me in terms of learning Algonquin. Although he understood the three languages quite well, he was slightly deaf and Algonquin came through to him a little better. So I spoke to him often in the Indian language.

Much of my learning of the language had been with my nose in the old missionary grammar and dictionary, books that had been compiled long ago. Basil observed, "You speak Indian like they did a million years ago!"

Mary was invariably a good teacher. She was patient whenever I tried to speak to her in Algonquin, always answering me in that language if I initiated the conversation.

I looked around for tasks to make myself useful, passing up mowing the lawn and painting the porch as being tasks anyone could do. Instead I chose a preeminently stinky job that stood out clearly as a golden opportunity to make my way. Mary was preparing to scrape some moose hide to make some babiche (a French word now passed into Canadian English), long thongs of raw hide used to lace snowshoes.

In the fall of the year during moose hunting season, hunters often brought moose hide to the Commandas to be tanned and used for babiche. Even in the spring there were quarter hides lying about.

As I stood curiously by outside, Mary was picking over one of the hides that had been soaking in water.

"You know," I said, "I'd like to learn how to do that."

"You would?" she said incredulously. She had never heard of anyone wanting to learn a job with as little appeal as that one. "I'll be glad to show you."

She took a quarter moose hide from the water and draped it over the *tcicakwahiganâtik*, a log about five feet long. One end of the log was propped up on two legs and the other end went down to the ground.

"Here, you take this knife like this and you cut the hairs off." She cut along the surface of the skin. "Don't cut the skin itself or it won't come out right. Those roots of the hair you have to get out by scraping."

I cut some of the hair.

"We used to use this hair, after we cleaned it, in pillows and mattresses, but we don't do that anymore."

The job became difficult when it came to scraping the hide. After all the hairs were cut, I scraped the roots of the moose hair and then, on the meat side of the skin, I scraped the sinew from the hide. This job was so much more difficult than cutting and splitting wood, for instance, that it hardly bore comparison. The stink that rose from a moose hide that had been lying around and then soaking for a while was terrible.

Mary made me an apron using a cord and a plastic garbage bag. When our hands got dirty they smelled, and the smell would not go from clothes until they were washed.

It was not hard to keep warm while scraping a moose hide. In the early spring with the temperature sometimes forty-five degrees, I could get a moose hide quarter from the water, put it over the scraping log, and work outside in my undershirt, quite confident that in a few minutes or so I would be warm.

Day-to-day life in the household was invariably interesting. I tried to take advantage of opportunities to learn. William appreciated having me scrape the moose hides as much as Mary did. I still did not know what would happen in terms of birchbark canoe making.

CHAPTER 7

The beginning of my apprenticeship in canoe building came suddenly. One day William said, "Do you want to get some bark?"

William and Mary and I drove forty miles north of Maniwaki in the pickup truck. We parked by the side of the highway and William handed me the axes. He carried the chainsaw himself. Mary stayed by the side of the road and said she would keep busy, even though we might be gone three or four hours.

William crossed the road and led the way up a fairly steep hill. I looked at the birch trees as we made our way through the woods, but I didn't see any that looked promising. We stopped at the top of the ridge.

"I was back here last summer. I think there are some good trees a ways ahead. We ought to be able to find a good one."

The words took me back to the birchbark canoe I saw the white man building on Lake Superior. Although the canoe was about sixteen feet long, no single bark sheet had been larger than about four feet by four feet. The bark sheets had been taken from smaller birch trees and were sewn together with spruce root.

The fourteen-foot canoe in William's shop had, on the other hand, been made with a single sheet of birchbark. We were now going to look for a tree big enough to provide such a sheet.

As I followed William through the woods, the birch trees we saw were bigger and bigger.

"Look at that one over there," William said, taking a slightly different tack through the woods. We walked up to an enormous birch tree. I had never seen one so large.

He put his hand on the trunk and walked part way around. "No good," he said. "See the trunk? It curves off to the side. I didn't see that from back there. We'll have to leave it." He picked up the chainsaw and started off with me following and looking back at the largest birch tree I had ever seen.

As we walked, his head turned first to one side and then the other, trying to spot a big birch through the leafy branches of the trees around us. With the ax, William cut off a little strip of bark around the trunk of one tree.

"You see," he said. "This is what you do when you get to a tree that looks promising. Take a piece off like this and then bend it. If it doesn't crack, it's all right. Some of the bark is dry. That's no good in a canoe. You can't take the first big birch tree you come to. Then you have to make sure that the layers of the bark do not come apart when you bend and twist it. If they come apart on this little piece, they will come apart in the canoe. We call that *pitockwai*. Also, check to see that the eyes [latitudinal lines called lenticels] do not open up. These things will let water in your canoe. In some bark, they all open up. But don't take that kind of bark."

Finally he found a good tree. It was about eighteen inches in diameter at the butt. The trunk was straight and knot-free for more than fifteen feet.

We cleared away the brush around the base of the tree. Then

William started the saw and cut down two medium-sized nearby spruce trees. He directed me to place one under the birch where the butt of the tree would fall and the other one where the first branch would hit the ground.

"We can't let that trunk hit the ground. It would hit a rock or a stump for sure. We may not see a rock down there, but that trunk is going to find one. Then you've got a hole in the canoe."

When we were ready to cut the tree, I motioned that I would take the chainsaw but William wanted to cut the tree himself.

The huge birch came crashing down on its makeshift bed, crushing the two spruce trees into the ground. William cut a sixteen-foot log that rested on the spruce supports. Then, again using the chainsaw, he made a cut the entire length of the log to a depth of about half an inch, going through the bark and just into the wood.

"Here," he said, handing me an ax, "take this. Now we've got to pry the bark off the tree. Start at the cut and peel it back on both sides."

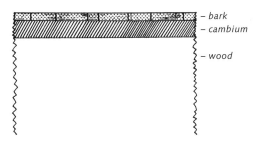

– bark
– cambium
– wood

Cross-section of birch tree

I had peeled flimsy little bark from birch before for fires and just for the fun of it, but this canoe bark was a revelation. It was a quarter of an inch thick and obviously a tough material. It would be easier to cut strong canvas than this piece of canoe bark.

William Commanda carrying a roll of birchbark with a tumpline.

I came to a spot where the bark was difficult to remove.

"Wait!" William said. "Let me get that. That's going to put a hole in the bark if you go too fast."

After more than an hour, a very large sheet of bark was nearly off the trunk, but the heavy birch log was still holding the bark sheet against the two spruce logs. William cut two small birch saplings, and we used them to lever the big log off the spruce.

Soon the bark sheet was free. It was four and a half feet wide and fifteen feet long. We lifted it back on top of the log and carefully rolled the bark, white side in, tawny side out, and then tied it with rope.

I carried the large roll of birchbark out of the woods. William still had charge of the chainsaw. The whole operation had taken almost four hours. Mary was a little distance into the woods when we got back. She had some plants in her hand.

"I found some medicine," she said as she came to meet us. She had made her trip worthwhile by doing some shopping, more or less.

◆

William and Mary had been making birchbark canoes for a number of years. While Mary came by the skill in a traditional way, William did not.

Mary and Basil's father, Charlie Smith, had made birchbark canoes all his life, although he was not particularly known as a canoe maker. Mary helped her father sew the spruce root on canoes from time to time. Photos of Charlie Smith making a birchbark canoe have been published a number of times in the United States.

William's father was not a birchbark canoe builder. In his community, canoe building was a skill passed on from father to son, but not all the men were canoe makers. He learned in the 1960s when he was chief of the band. At that time, representatives from museums and movie companies were coming regularly to Maniwaki in search of birchbark canoes. He was taught in part by his uncle who lived nearby, and in part by Mary's father who lived with them for a number of years.

Canoes were part of the youth of both William and Mary. Mary told of the time her mother was paddling across a lake in one of Charlie Smith's canoes. Mary was a young child and her little brother was also in the canoe. They came upon a deer swimming in the water. Their mother did not want to pass up a chance to add to the food supply, so she paddled over to the deer and hit it on the head with an ax. She grabbed the antlers with one hand and paddled with the other until they reached shore, all the while trying to keep the children quiet.

Mary also told of the time when she was young and living with her family in a log cabin on a river north of Maniwaki. They made trips often from the cabin. Her mother had to pack all the gear — blankets, tent, and food — in their sixteen-foot birchbark canoe. Four children, the hunting dog, and Mary's father, Charlie, also went in the canoe.

"Just before lunch my father would put out the fishing line from the canoe and most of the time we'd have fish for lunch. If my father killed a deer at one of our camping spots, we'd stay there for two or three days and my mother would make a little smoking rack with a birchbark cover over it to smoke the meat.

"My mother and father would always paddle the canoe. But my father made little paddles for the children and we would try to help out a little. My father never jumped the rapids with us. We always portaged. My father and mother always jumped the rapids alone."

Mary's mother would set up the tent for the night. The canvas tent had no floor but she cut balsam boughs and laid them down. Blankets went on top of the boughs. Her mother would bring a smudge pot into the tent to rid it of mosquitoes.

In the manner of many Indian women, Mary's mother was very retiring and shy. Her knowledge of French and English was not as good as her husband's. She would occasionally get mad at someone who did not speak Algonquin, and she had to work up a little imprecation of some sort. "Go to hell, please!" she would say.

Mary's father was called Kickanakwat (Broken Cloud) in Algonquin and Charlie Smith in English and French. He guided for missionaries as a young man, travelling by canoe with them to places as distant as two hundred miles in one direction and three hundred miles in another.

William's father had a birchbark canoe that he used for over thirty years. The family would take it up on the trapline for several months and bring it down when the rivers opened up. William himself had used a birchbark canoe until the 1930s.

Something that became more and more clear as I learned about birchbark canoes was that a man who built them was a very hard man to trap in the woods.

When William was young, he heard a story about an old Maniwaki Indian. The man had been up in the woods on his trapline. When he had loaded the canoe at the end of the season with his wife, gear, furs, and children, the water came to within an inch of the gunwales. He told his wife that he would make another canoe, so he took some gear from the canoe and sent her on her way back to the reserve. He started early that morning and finished at four the next morning, using nails to save much time. When he was finished, he had a serviceable twelve-foot canoe and made his way back to Maniwaki.

William and I headed for the woods once again in search of material. This time we went eighty miles north to a stand of cedar. William cut down a cedar with no knots on the trunk for fifteen feet.

"Cedar is hell to split if there is a knot in it, but not hard at all if there is not," he explained.

With a mallet and steel wedges, we split the long log in half, into quarters, and then again. He then cut five-foot lengths from other trees for the canoe's ribs. These lengths were also split several times. The operation was not as delicate as getting the birchbark had been, but was attended by swarms of blackflies and mosquitoes.

Once our work was done and the wood was in the truck, William took out the sandwiches and tea Mary had prepared for us, and we dined on the tailgate of the truck. There were fewer flies and mosquitoes in the open area of the dirt bush road than there had been in the woods.

"It's nice to get ahead on some of that long cedar," William said. "I've got some at home but you can always use more. We might build several canoes this summer and you can help us if you want."

I was not about to question an offer like that.

Our next trip was with Mary. We went more than a hundred miles to the northeast along the Gatineau River to an abandoned Indian settlement. There was a clearing there that had been a large potato field. Tall black spruce grew in the field and their roots were not tangled with those of other trees.

Each of us had an ax. A few feet from the base of a spruce tree, we dug at the ground with the back of the ax. The roots were several inches below the surface. As soon as we found one, we cut it with the ax and pulled it out of the ground and away from the tree. If the root went under another root, we fed the first one under the second and continued with it, coming back for the other one later.

After about an hour we had a good pile of root, some pieces as long as twenty feet. We rolled these into a twenty-five-pound "dough-nut," which I carried back to the truck.

The first materials I helped collect were not, as it turned out, for a canoe that I would help build. William had received a call from the National Capital Commission in Ottawa. The first Canada Canoe Festival in Ottawa was being planned and the organizers wanted to hire William to make a birchbark canoe. This wasn't the first such request.

In 1975, the Department of Indian Affairs funded a class in Amos, Quebec, for fifteen Algonquin students to learn birchbark canoe construction. William and Mary taught the class. They made twelve birchbark canoes there that summer. Canoes built by the Commandas have also ended up in museum collections in Canada, the United States, Japan, Poland, Denmark, Germany, and France.

William and Mary often demonstrated the making of birchbark canoes as well. They had constructed birchbark canoes in many places, among them Washington, D.C., during the United States bicentennial celebrations; Toronto, for the Canadian National Exhibition; and at Man and His World, the former Expo '67, in Montreal.

Someone from the festival was to meet William in Maniwaki and talk it over. For some reason, this meeting brought to my mind first contacts, in the present day, between whites and Indians.

White people live all their lives with preconceptions about Indians. Even if they were well disposed toward Indians – and not part of that other group of whites with a decidedly different view – it was interesting to see the reactions of first-time white visitors to the Commanda household.

There was usually an apprehension just below the surface and an almost visible relief when they saw the colour television and the automatic coffee maker. I saw over and over again how much more enthusiastic whites were about accepting people of Indian origin when the latter lived as whites rather than Indians. And when an Indian had a close white friend, more often than not they were doing "white things" with each other, rather than Indian activities.

This sort of feeling on the part of whites has an interesting corollary that causes the poor Indians to be pushed both ways. Such happens when those with an interest in Indian culture feel that the Indians are not being Indian enough.

Much later, in 1980 when my book, *The Indian Crafts of William and Mary Commanda*, was published, a young admirer of Indian culture was paging through the book. "Bermuda shorts!" he exclaimed suddenly, frightening me, as I had no idea what it was that excited him. "Bermuda shorts! What's an Indian doing wearing Bermuda shorts?" I took the book from him and, to be sure, there in my own book was a photo of William splitting cedar for a *tikinâgan* – and wearing Bermuda shorts. Then the import of it all hit me: in the long and fruitful history of North American Indian ethnography, ethnologists and others had written about Indians and photographed them, but there was possibly no other photograph of an Indian wearing Bermuda shorts, Edward Curtis's pioneering work notwithstanding. And I had taken the photo.

◆

William took a good roll of birchbark from the stock he had on hand, as well as some spruce root and cedar. We made a couple of trips to Ottawa to deliver the materials. Then he and Mary spent two weeks at the festival making the canoe and answering questions about Indian crafts and culture.

Invariably a visitor would come up to William, as he was the one of the two who did not seem to be working. "You see," William would start by way of explanation, "in the Indian culture, the woman does all the work. So here Mary does all the sewing and the rest of the work and I answer the questions." The visitor laughed at the joke, as did William and Mary.

CHAPTER 8

A few weeks after the Commandas returned from the Ottawa exhibition, they began construction of a birchbark canoe at home. First they had to prepare the materials. To make it more pliable, the big roll of birchbark was submerged in a tub of water for a few days. If it had not been soaked, it would have been brittle, and there were a few times during the building process when it might have cracked. In any case, it would have been harder to work with.

The preparation of the spruce root was easy work, but slow. The ideal root was the diameter of a pencil, or maybe a little larger. It was soaked for a day so that it would be easy to work with. When it was wet, the thin bark of the root came off fairly easily. Then a split was started at the thick end of the root with a small knife cut. The root was split evenly along its length, which could be as long as fifteen or twenty feet. If the split started to run to one side, the other half of the root was pulled until the split evened up. Although the technique was different, preparing spruce root reminded me of knitting. The work was easy and relaxing, if time-consuming.

Once a length of root was split, both halves were sometimes split again to be rid of the middle of the root. After a long root was split, it was again rolled into a coil. It could then be left to dry and soaked again before it was used. In fact, once gathered, the materials used in the building of a birchbark canoe can be left to dry indefinitely. All that is necessary to get them in top shape is to soak them in water. The versatility of the primary materials of the Indians never ceased to amaze me.

We built the canoe in the Commandas' workshop next to the house. The old Indian tools sufficed in most cases. William split the cedar gunwales by hand, as he did the ribs and sheathing.

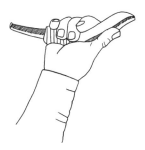

An Indian crooked knife

William had made five or six crooked knives. These were the Indian tools *par excellence*. The handle bent away from the carver. The blade curved up on the end and was good for carving out hollows. William made the blades either from old files or from an old bandsaw blade of particularly hard steel. As it turned out, even though the crooked knife was the most important tool in the Indian manufacture of the birchbark canoe, he rarely used it, preferring the drawknife instead.

The drawknife was an old settler's tool, nothing more than a straight blade with handles on each end perpendicular to the blade. The carver pulls the blade toward himself. The tool was often employed for taking bark from logs. William used it to make paddles and snowshoe frames as well as gunwales, ribs, and the sheathing for birchbark canoes after these wooden components had been split.

I worked with the drawknife but did not find it easy to use at first. I had a tendency to pull it directly toward me with the blade perpendicular to the line of pull. The idea was to pull the knife in a straight line but with the blade at an angle. The cutting was smoother that way.

In Aboriginal times, and even until a generation ago, the tools were much more primitive. Holes were made in the bark with a triangular bone awl. Mary remembered using such tools when she was young. Holes in wood were made using a type of awl with a bow that made it rotate. In fact, it looked much like the assembly the Indians used for starting a fire. And when the ribs were split, not by cutting as is done today, they were finished by abrasion with stones or shells.

Felling trees presented an interesting challenge to the Indians centuries ago. They chopped a girdle around the tree with a stone ax or an adz. Above this girdle, they applied mud or clay. At the base of the tree, they built a fire that would char the trunk but not burn anything above the level of the mud or clay. They then removed the char with the ax or adz and repeated the process until the tree fell.

Although the Indian benefited from the use of steel tools, the coming of the white man brought about a bastardization of the construction of the birchbark canoe. As early as the nineteenth century, it was common to see gunwales and gunwale caps held together by nails. It is not hard to understand why; nails saved a lot of labour. Binding gunwales with spruce root was very time-consuming, even though spruce root was more effective than nails.

We soon fell into a work routine. Mary got up and made breakfast. William, Basil, and I rose and ate about eight o'clock. Basil was so retiring that he always ate in the living room, whether there was room at the table or not.

During the course of the day, Basil would often wander through the shop to see how the project was getting on. As often as not, Mary and I would be working on the canoe and William would be talking to a passerby from the highway who had seen the birchbark canoe in progress and had stopped to talk. Then we would overhear from William stories that we had heard many times before, and occasionally a new one.

One day a visitor said, "My wife has a very expensive fur coat and she dropped it on the floor so that now there is a big grease stain. Did the Indians have a way of getting that kind of thing off fur?" And he stood there watching us work on the canoe.

"Oh, of course!" William said. "Tomato juice."

"Tomato juice?" the man asked.

"Yes," William said. "Do you have a fifty-gallon barrel?"

"No, but I guess I could get one."

"Well," William explained very carefully, "you fill that barrel with tomato juice and then put the coat in it. After a few days, it will be as good as new."

At that point, Basil burst out laughing and, I think, spoiled the recipe.

◆

Basil was the epitome of the old Indian trapper. One could see in him the heritage of the primordial Algonquin who loved to roam about in the woods — indeed, needed to — hunting and trapping, and who continued to do this even when agricultural Native groups to the south were well along the way to adopting the white man's way of life.

In good physical shape, Basil was particularly sociable and extremely well liked. He was not averse to having a glass of beer, so one night the two of us went to a tavern in town. Now a number of these places had a reputation for being rough spots, the town itself being a bit of a frontier village. Some people went to the hotels as much to fight as to drink. And sometimes the situation would get out of hand. Basil and I, both being of pacific natures, ordinarily preferred to stay away from such commotion.

But it was time for a night out, so we went to a local tavern, sat down, and ordered a couple of beers. Sure enough, it happened. We had been talking about fifteen minutes (I was shouting nearly to the point of hysteria, not only because of Basil's partial deafness but also to be heard above the music) when all hell broke loose. Two bad fights broke out simultaneously. One man was after another who was slightly drunker than himself, landing solid kicks and punches on the chest. I couldn't believe ribs weren't being broken. The other two were going at each other with chairs and throwing wild punches at those who were trying to stop them. Basil and I quickly crawled under our table and said three Hail Marys.

Three of Basil's finest qualities were his alertness, resourcefulness, and sense of humour. We drove home later that evening in a pounding rain. My decrepit truck had lousy windshield wipers, to add to a lengthy list of other shortcomings, so that I had to hunch over to see through the windshield. On the passenger's side, Basil was hunched over slightly in empathy.

Just then my wiper quit while his was still going strong. "Pass me the wheel," he said, quick to offer any help that might be useful.

◆

In William's workshop, the canoe was coming along. I was mesmerized by the work, and William was accommodating in his explanations to me.

Birchbark canoes were built directly on the ground under a canopy made of saplings and birchbark sheets. Birchbark dries after a short while and cannot be worked unless it is very pliable, so the canopy was necessary to shade the material from the hot sun.

Years ago, stakes were stuck in the ground to hold up the sides of the canoe. In the last century, building forms became common, which allowed several canoes to be constructed with a minimum of inconvenience. A building platform was made by joining boards together, and was about four feet wide and sixteen feet long, depending on the size of the canoe.

William set his platform on carpenter's horses in the shop. Holes he had drilled in the platform received the stakes that would hold up the sides of the canoe.

The roll of bark, which had been soaked in an old bathtub for several days, was unrolled, exterior side up, on the building platform. The sheet of bark we were to use was impressive, about twenty feet long and more than four feet wide. We were going to make a canoe fifteen and a half feet long, so we cut the bark at about the sixteen-foot mark. Because the bark was not quite wide enough, the extra bark would be used to fill out each side up to the gunwales.

When the bark was spread out on the platform, we centred a plywood frame the same size as the gunwales on top of it, weighting the frame with heavy stones. Some builders used the inside gunwales for this purpose, raising the gunwales later to their final position.

When the bark was well weighted down, five gores were cut on each side of the bark and the sides were turned up. Next, the inner gunwale frame and the outwales were put in place. The birch stakes were then placed in their holes to hold the sides of the canoe up and to hold the gunwales in position. The thing now had the rough form of a canoe, although at this stage a passerby would probably not have been impressed.

William made some measurements to make sure that the gunwales were the proper height, both amidships and at the ends. He held the gunwales in place with temporary clamps.

Then we began what had always been Mary's specialty. She was the one in charge of sewing the gunwales. We trimmed the bark even with the top of the gunwales. William had marked the gunwales off in two-inch sections. Every other section was bound with spruce root. The ribs would fit into the gunwale from beneath in the remaining unbound sections.

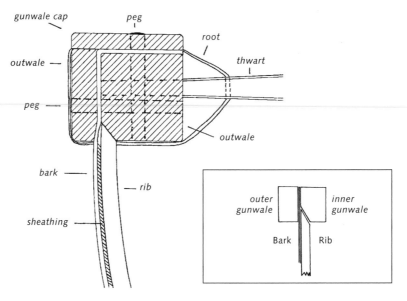

Cross-section of birchbark canoe gunwale

At each spot that had to be bound, we drilled five holes through the bark just below the gunwales. We then passed the spruce root around the gunwales ten times, twice through each hole. There were perhaps fifty or sixty intervals along the gunwales where they had to be bound. It was not a difficult job, but the work was long. When it was finished, the bark was sandwiched tightly between the two cedar gunwales. Spruce root stretches slightly when wet so that it dried tight, and I found it bound our structure more tightly than if nails had been used.

For the ribs, William used the cedar pieces we had already partially split in the woods. Using a froe to split them further, he always started at the small end and worked toward the butt. He continued doing this until he got the rough form of the rib — three-eighths of an inch thick and two inches wide — and then, using a drawknife, he finished them on a carving horse. Shaped something like a carpenter's horse, the carving horse has an arm in the centre that holds the wood so both hands can be used on the drawknife. Once William had made a bundle of the ribs, he soaked them for several days.

The sheathing was more thinly split than the ribs and was two to three times as wide. These pieces were also soaked in water.

Next we began to form the ends of the canoe.

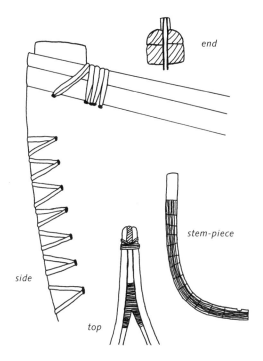

Canoe bow and stem-piece

William cut the bark to the curvature he wanted. The bow design is the most important characteristic that distinguishes the canoes of one Native group from those of another. Ojibway canoes, for instance, traditionally had a bow that was greater than a semicircle, whereas the Algonquin stem-piece pointed roughly straight up. Some groups had other variations. A low bow might be employed when the canoeist wanted to go along streams with overhanging branches. Canoes may also have been built that way to avoid taking too much wind on open lakes. Different builders within the same group often had slightly varying ways of making a bow, although they generally followed the traditional pattern of the Native group to which they belonged. One canoe maker's work could usually be recognized easily by another canoe maker. A canoe builder might employ various techniques at different times in his career.

After William had cut the bow out of the bark, he fashioned a triangular piece of cedar about three feet long. This was to be the stem-piece. This he split lengthwise four times, leaving it tied at one end. The splits would make the cedar piece easier to bend. It was then steamed for a few minutes and bent to the desired bow curvature. William tied it in that shape to dry.

When the stem-piece was dry, William fitted it into the bow and clamped it temporarily in place. Mary's work then began again. She sewed the cedar stem-piece to the bark with spruce root, her careful stitching making a very decorative bow.

After the stem-piece was well sewn in, the gunwale ends were bent up slightly and joined to it. Back from the bow, a headboard was added to shoulder the two gunwales and give added support to the stem-piece.

The canoe was not far from being completed. The hull was shaped, the gunwales were placed and bound with spruce root. There remained three operations: the ribs and sheathing had to be put in place, the gunwale caps had to be pegged to the gunwales, and the whole canoe had to be gummed.

I didn't pass up the chance to add to my Algonquin vocabulary while helping William and Mary build this canoe. They coached me on the names of the various canoe parts. A few of the words were mercifully easy to learn, such as *wâgina* for rib, or *otâkan* for bow. Others were

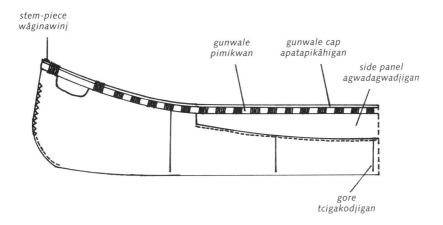

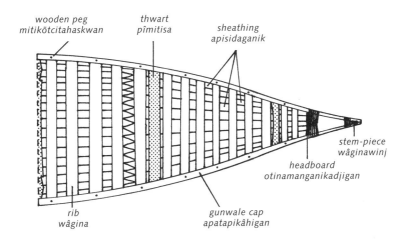

Parts of a birchbark canoe (English and Algonquin), side and top views

so long as to strike fear into the hearts of the most intrepid. *Apatapikâhigan* is the name for the gunwale cover. The headboard is called *otinamanganikadjigan* and the stem of the canoe is *onakojaonek nimitamônak*.

The rest of my Algonquin vocabulary expanded as well. Some of the words had interesting figurative meanings. A young woman told me about the word *ningasimonike*. It means, generally and literally, "he's building a tent." One figurative meaning is that the fellow has an erection in his pants.

Ideally, all of the parts of the canoe should be prefinished. Before anything is joined together, the spruce root should be prepared and split and the ribs and sheathing split and laid out. That way, when construction begins, the operation is basically a process of fitting the pieces together.

However, we still had some preparation to do. William had to finish the ribs on the carving horse, and Mary still needed to taper the pieces of sheathing with a knife. All these pieces were submerged in water, then William steamed them in his steaming box. Made out of sheet metal, this box measured about eight feet long by eight inches square. It had a heater rigged to it so that water inside could be heated to boiling just by plugging the heater in. It was one of those modern conveniences the Indians didn't have centuries ago.

The ribs were steamed, two at a time, for about five minutes. Then they were taken out, bent over the knee in two places, and fitted into the canoe. When two ribs were bent together, one on top of the other, they could be set amidships in the canoe. Then the top rib could be moved one spot closer to the end. Since the canoe narrowed toward the ends, the top rib fitted very well at the next position.

After the ribs were all fitted into the canoe, they were left to dry. When dry, they could be taken out and laid aside while the sheathing was carefully placed, overlapping the pieces to cover the entire inner hull right up to the gunwales. The ribs were then put back over the sheathing and it was only at this time that the rib ends were carved to fit under the inner gunwale.

When this was done, William fitted the gunwale cover – almost like a cedar gunwale turned on its side – over each gunwale. He secured the covers by driving square hardwood pegs into the gunwales.

At this stage, a birchbark canoe is reasonably impervious to water. However, it is still necessary to seal it completely with spruce gum.

Pieces of hard gum are gathered from the wounds in spruce trees. It takes a great deal of gathering because the builder might get very little from a single tree. Once he has a nice panful, he melts it down, skimming the impurities (dirt or flecks of wood) from the surface. Fat is then added as a tempering agent to ensure that the mixture does not run in the sun when it is hot, or crack in the cold.

The gum is applied on the two ends of the canoe, at all seams, and at any points along the hull where it appears there might be a small hole.

When the gumming was done, our canoe was finished.

Sometimes the canoe needed a slight bit of additional gumming while the canoeist was away from home. Often the canoeist carried a small tin gum pot hung by a short wire in the bow of the canoe. This pot contained gum that had been tempered at home. Because it hardened in the pot, the gum couldn't fall out. If a leak developed in the canoe, the pot would be put over a little fire and the gum melted so that it could be applied to the trouble spot on the canoe. The remainder of the gum hardened again in the pot.

If the canoeist had not brought a gum pot along, he could take a few hard knobs of spruce gum from a tree. These he chewed until they were soft, then applied the gum to the canoe.

It was Mary who did most of the gumming on our canoe. It was not too difficult a job, but it had to be done well, or later the canoe would leak.

A few days after the canoe was completed, William and I took it to a lake several miles away for a tryout.

The Commandas had a cabin by the side of a small bay on the lake. We launched the canoe in front of their cabin. We paddled the birchbark canoe, which seemed more buoyant than a regular canoe, across the quiet bay silently and with ease. William was in the stern and I in the bow. He paid careful attention to the bottom of the canoe to see if there might be any leaks. Two small trickles of water soon appeared.

We took the canoe to shore and turned it over. William looked around for the spot at which he saw the first leak. He found a tiny hole no larger than a pinhole through the gum. He tested it by putting his mouth to the bark and sucking. If he could draw air, there was the hole. He told me to follow his lead in order to learn the procedure.

The gum was hard, so to close the hole he lit a match and held it to the spot. The surrounding gum soon softened, enabling him to push it over the hole with his thumb. He repaired the other small leak in like fashion.

When we were out on the water once again, our canoe was leak free and likely to remain that way for a long time.

Participating in the making of a birchbark canoe was a vivid experience for me. It epitomized in some way the fascination of Indian culture. Again I thought what a difference between a commercial canoe — sometimes also a thing of beauty — and this canoe, of which the design was probably unchanged for centuries, if not millennia. The difference was one of life and feeling.

I could not wait to work on more canoes — and eventually, to build my own.

CHAPTER 9

A whole new botanical world was opening up to me in Maniwaki. I had come to the Commandas' household hoping to learn about birchbark canoe making. To make a birchbark canoe was a rather complicated task; I had not expected it to be easy. At the same time, I had not expected to be so overwhelmed by other aspects of the culture.

When Mary went into the woods, it was as if she was going into a pharmacy. Mary always left an offering in the woods when taking medicine from nature. It might be a little bit of tobacco or only a penny. She got much of the medicine in the fall. She dried it and kept it indefinitely. Her list of medicines was long. Some of the names she knew in English or French, but many she knew only in Algonquin.

Many Algonquin, especially the women, had a great store of knowledge of medicinal herbs. This knowledge, much as the language, was dying out fast. An anthropologist had collected a good deal of information from Maniwaki residents in the 1960s. It would be impossible for her to collect so much information now, as the majority of the people who had helped her had died.

I had a chance to meet the anthropologist when she visited Maniwaki. Her experience in gathering botanical information from several Algonquin communities in the early 1960s had been a unique one.

Her information on the plants of the Algonquin had gone into her doctoral dissertation. It had not been published, but it appeared that it would be in the near future and that the publication would be in an academic format.

She told me about her experience a decade and a half earlier gathering information on the use of plants by the Algonquin. A lot of people she worked with could not speak any English or French.

Although eager to learn more about plants, I was a bit uncertain about my ability to assimilate any more information for the moment. My absorbing interest in the Algonquin language and in birchbark canoe making was about all I could handle. Even so, I knew I wanted to see her information some day – and soon.

I began to realize that if she had written her dissertation in a scientific vernacular it might not be so easy for me to understand. Also, it seemed clear that a popular book on the subject, as opposed to an anthropological treatise, might be more useful in passing the botanical information on to the next Algonquin generation.

I asked her if she had considered putting the material she had gathered into a popular format.

"I couldn't do that," she said. "I was given this information freely; I wouldn't want to profit from it."

She didn't mention, though, whether or not she thought that a doctoral dissertation was a form of profit.

◆

Many times people asked Mary for a medicine for some ailment. On one occasion, a clerk in the local department store came to the house and asked if Mary had something for baldness. She gave him a small container of bear grease and told him how to apply it.

Mary harvested *kapisibunkweiak* to alleviate weakness. *Ozawadjíbik* (yellow root) was good for liver ailments, particularly hepatitis. The most common bush tea among the Algonquin, and one that white people in the area occasionally used, was Labrador tea, which was called *muckikobak*. Mary used *wikenj* (calamus) for coughs, colds, and cramps. She shredded the root and put it in boiling water to steep. For fever and piles she used *cikakwack*. When Mary had a bad cough, she chewed a root called *tipwebanodjíbik* and swallowed the juice.

Once, when I had cut my leg, Mary gave me some balsam gum to put on the cut. There was a slight swelling, and the balsam gum seemed to draw out the pus.

One of the white doctors in Maniwaki, long since dead, had sometimes recommended to the Indians that they return home and take their own medicines. He appears to have been the only doctor in town who had much faith in Indian medicine.

◆

Another rapidly disappearing craft was the tanning of a full-size moose hide. The more I learned about it, the more evident it became that making Indian crafts was anything but a quiet, pastoral undertaking.

Mary had continued to do smoke tanning yearly. Every fall she went through the tough scraping and tanning process. As she reached her sixties, the scraping got to be too much for her, although she was still able to do the tanning.

Tanning and making babiche were arduous tasks. William once commented as he walked past me when I was scraping, "You know, that was woman's work." I handed him the scraper, but he walked off. All those women who had worked at the chore for centuries had my deepest respect. Scraping hides required great perseverance and strength. Of all the Indian crafts made today, those that necessitate scraping hides are the least popular – to the makers, that is.

Smoke-tanned deer and moose hide is sought after by Indians and connoisseurs of Indian craft because it is so difficult to produce. If you see Indian-produced moccasins, coats, or mittens, the odds are great that they are made of factory-tanned hides. Factory-tanned hides are produced at reasonable rates by a number of suppliers. Mary sometimes bought smoke-tanned hide – if it was available. It rarely was. As cultural assimilation continued to take place, smoke tanning was one of the first aspects of Native material culture to disappear.

Rapid Lake, an Algonquin reserve located ninety miles north of Maniwaki, is much smaller than the Maniwaki reserve. Because of its isolation and other factors, the Indians there all retained Algonquin as their first language. They also kept most of the traditional skills, although these were dying out. At the settlement, a number of women continued to tan hides. Often one of the women would bring a partially tanned hide to Mary, who would buy it.

Mary enlisted me to scrape a large moose hide for tanning – one of the most forlorn, thankless jobs one could imagine. For William, I was a cultural anomaly, a curiosity. "For centuries, the Indian was a slave to the white man. Now we have a white man who is a slave to the Indians," he told a visitor while I was hard at work.

I scraped the hide using a couple of different tools, neither of them rendering the job particularly easy. A straight, dull-edged knife required full force, but because it was dull, there was little chance of cutting the hide. A sharp drawknife made the work much easier, but one had to be careful not to cut completely through the skin.

When the hide was scraped, Mary and I made a large, four-sided stretching rack of hardwood saplings. This rack was a little larger than the hide and was either leaned up against something or held a few feet off the ground on forked sticks. I then cut holes around the perimeter of the scraped hide and passed a long rope through the holes and around the edge of the rack. Soon the hide was stretched tight. My next job was to beat the hell out of it with a dull instrument similar to a garden hoe. This beating went on for hours and loosened up the hide. Every fifteen minutes or so, my work would stop until the rope was tightened again. In this way, the hide stretched and softened as it slowly dried. Had it been left simply to dry, it would have been hard and useless.

After six stretching and drying stints, I put the hide in soapy lukewarm water. The laundry soap was added to the water as a softening agent and worked very well in lieu of the animals' brains that the early Indians had used. The beating and soaking process was repeated until the hide was soft, dry, and nearly white.

Once the moose hide was tanned, it had to be smoked to give it a good colour. It was folded over a smoldering fire of dead wood for about half an hour. The smoking gave the hide a lovely tawny colouring, which deepened the longer the hide was smoked. It also gave it a smoky aroma. Care had to be taken to let the smoke do its job without bringing the hide too close to heat, or it would have been cooked and stiff.

My enthusiasm for scraping and tanning hides solidly cemented my reputation in the neighbourhood as an eccentric. By then, I had been on the reserve more than a year. The fact that a white man would want to learn the Algonquin language baffled most of the people. Of what use was it? To get ahead in the world, one had to use English. (This was also a strong tenet of the English in Canada, especially when it was a question of French-speaking people.) That a white man wanted to learn how to make a birchbark canoe was perhaps more understandable. It was, after all, an impressive craft and produced a tangible thing that brought attention and money. But scraping and tanning moose hides was something no one in his right mind would want to do, so I was, ipso facto, not all there.

CHAPTER 10

Canoe making was not a constant activity at the Commanda household, but matters relating to the canoe were frequently talked about.

Some of William's young adulthood had been spent as a hunting and fishing guide at a large wilderness camp about forty miles from Maniwaki. The canoe had been his most important tool, and up to the 1930s, he had frequently used a birchbark canoe. Guides took fishermen on canoe trips that often lasted several days. They would portage from a large main lake to smaller lakes or follow rivers more than one hundred miles from the main lake.

In the 1930s, when a large American-owned lumber company was paying one dollar a day for workers, the hunting and fishing camp was paying guides three dollars a day and the Indian women who worked as cook one dollar a day. The Indians reminisce about those days as if they were an idyllic time. Difficult circumstances, though, are also remembered.

Mary recounted the story of a particularly cantankerous tourist.

Indians portaging birchbark canoes as tourists carry loads with tumplines, c. 1920.

He went out for a day's fishing with one of the guides and tormented the poor Indian from morning till dusk. "Paddle this way; come back a little. How come we aren't getting any fish? Why are the mosquitoes so bad?" After such a stream of babble, the guide quit when he arrived back at the camp. It was no small matter for a guide to quit a job like that, given the local economic situation. Another man was assigned to the problem tourist with the same result. The same thing happened to a third guide.

The guide foreman readily recognized the seriousness of the problem. His solution was to assign Mary's brother Romeo to the impossible tourist. Romeo went off happily with the man for many days and came back without a complaint. Romeo had been born with a hearing impairment.

Indian guides with white fishermen in the 1920s in two Algonquin birchbark canoes. Algonquin birchbark canoes were used extensively by Indian fishing guides until the Second World War.

The stories revolving around the birchbark canoe were legion. I came to learn of birchbark canoes that had been in constant use for over forty years. Later I paddled a canoe that had been constructed fifty years earlier, and it seemed to be in as good shape as the day it was made.

◆

I left the Commanda household at the end of November and set up shop at a hunting and fishing camp fifteen miles east of Maniwaki. There I was able to write and read, study the Algonquin language when I could summon the discipline, and lace snowshoes to earn some money.

About every two weeks I returned to town for supplies and for a visit to William, Mary, and Basil. I usually arrived early in the morning and on occasion Mary had fresh bread, coffee, and home-baked beans. William and Mary both enjoyed sitting and visiting over coffee, sometimes for hours at a time.

◆

William sat on the davenport, his hands resting between his knees, facing me on the davenport opposite him. We had been talking about a variety of things. There was a pause. Then he spoke in a tone of entreaty that was quite foreign to him.

"Do you suppose you could write a book about me?" he asked.

It was a strange idea. I had written mostly novels. I was intensely interested in Indian culture but I had never thought about writing a book on the subject. Nor did it ever occur to me that William was thinking about a book. I did not know what to say. I went back to the hunting and fishing camp, thinking over his strange request. It was the only time I could recall that he had asked someone for something.

Two weeks later I was back in town. "Do you remember asking me if I wanted to write a book about you?" I said. "What kind of book did you have in mind?"

"Well, I thought it would be nice to have a book about me and Mary and the crafts we make. You know, the birchbark canoe and snowshoes and Mary's tanning and things like that."

William and Mary had many practices worth emulating. Mary, in selling her crafts, wanted to avoid the evils of inflation. "When I travel somewhere," she said to me one time, "I don't like to pay a lot for crafts. So I keep prices for my own crafts low."

I had never met anyone as good as William was about visiting old people, whether they were in the hospital or at home. Visiting hospitalized people — French, English, or Indian — was probably his highest social priority. William and Mary also helped out Rapid Lake Natives who were in Maniwaki and in one sort of difficult position or another.

After this visit to William, I returned to my place in the woods and again mulled over his intriguing idea. The Commandas were versatile in the crafts they made, although they were not necessarily the best exponents of a given craft. William's nationalist views could probably be worked into a book in a way that would give it dimension. If a writer could reflect the sense of humour that William and Mary so often exhibited, it would give life to the book. As a sort of biography/how-to book, it might be an interesting project.

I wrote to an editor at McGraw-Hill Ryerson, a publishing company in Toronto. Recently she had rejected a novel of mine with such a courteous, laudatory letter that I thought perhaps she might like the project. She asked for an outline and sample chapter, which I wrote, showed to William, and sent to her. My proposal was approved and a contract was signed. We waited only for warm weather to get our project under way.

In the meantime, at the cabin I was studying the Algonquin grammar and the Algonquin dictionary. I noticed a strange effect that I had seen only once before.

During my stay on the reserve, I had an intense exposure to the Algonquin language and to native speakers – or at least it was as intense as I could make it. Now, in the woods, that immersion was removed. Even so, on a return visit to Maniwaki Mary said to me, "Who are you talking to out there? Your Algonquin has improved."

It reminded me of something that had happened when I was at university in France. For months I had been studying the French language. When I took a long vacation in eastern Europe, the surprising result was that my French improved. Then, as was now the case with Algonquin, it felt as though prolonged exposure to the language, followed by a period without hearing it spoken, had a way of allowing the language to coalesce.

During this time of intense study of Algonquin, a friend went down for a job interview in Ottawa. Bilingualism was a requirement in many jobs. The interviewer asked if he were bilingual. He answered, "Yes, I speak English and Indian." He was told that didn't count.

Officials of the city of Ottawa decided to institute a policy more progressive than simple bilingualism, and worked out a system whereby callers to the city government could be served in one of twenty-two languages. If the caller knew even one word of English — the word for Swahili, Italian, Chinese, Hindi, or whatever his language was, he or she would be referred to a city employee who could speak that language.

The Ottawa newspaper decided to challenge the new system. It gathered a multitude of callers representing the different languages and found that, sure enough, the city of Ottawa could, as advertised, offer services in twenty-two different languages.

Both the Ottawa city government in its progressive program and the Ottawa newspaper in its diligent investigation had overlooked the Algonquin language, the first language of the area, and one still spoken by many residents of, and visitors to, the city.

Although the Indian language was completely ignored, there were some interesting attempts to clean up the English language. I came upon a memo from some agency of the federal government advising on proper terminology when dealing with Indians.

Totally unacceptable, it said, were "redskin," "scalping," "Uncle Tomahawk," "Indian-giver" and "brown white man." "Squaw" was supposed to be occasionally acceptable but not appropriate. Others, such as "brave," were acceptable in a historical context. "Massacre" was never acceptable when discussing an Indian victory over the white man.

It was not hard to see the effect of speaking to an Indian in his own language, particularly in the case of the more isolated Rapid Lake Algonquin from the north who came to town regularly. If one simply said a word as basic as *kwe*, which means "hello," the person would first be surprised at being spoken to in Indian by a white. Secondly, there would be visible changes on the person's face, progressing from a look of extreme shyness to one of comfort.

The whites in Maniwaki were generally quite open to Indians. This did not, however, include even a rudimentary knowledge of the language. Had all the people in town been instructed to say "*Kwe. Mino kijikat.* Hello. It's a fine day," the day would have been a little finer because the greeting would have indicated that we were no longer going to deny the existence of the splendorous Indian language through lack of use of it.

◆

William plunged into the project of the book with great enthusiasm. Before I came back from the hunting and fishing camp, I started doing some reading and taking notes on Indian crafts.

I returned that spring to the Commandas' house to room with Basil upstairs. In the basement, I improvised a little office with two tables, my typewriter, and two cardboard boxes for filing. I shared my office with snowshoes waiting to be laced, three deerskins that had been scraped but not tanned, and a large bear hide that Mary was preparing as a rug.

We took pictures of scraping hides, tanning, lacing snowshoes, making spoons out of burls and the curved base of trees, making birchbark baskets, sewing moccasins and hats and coats, and making the *tikinagân*, or baby carrier.

William was alert to any possible photo opportunity. "Come outside, he said one day, "Mary is roasting a moose nose. Maybe you want to get a picture of that."

Work on the birchbark canoe section of the Commanda book would be the final phase of our project. Right in the middle of our work, a renaissance took place in Maniwaki.

There were perhaps no more than ten Indian makers of the

Mary Commanda roasting a moose nose.

birchbark canoe in North America, where once there had been many hundreds among more than twenty Native groups. The majority of the remaining handful were — to my good fortune — located at Maniwaki and Rapid Lake, with a few others at Golden Lake, Ontario, and Manouan, Quebec.

Many of the old canoe makers had let their skill lie dormant while they had been working for years as guides, woodcutters, and fire rangers, and at a number of other jobs. Occasionally the skill would be reawakened, and one of the old canoe makers would start to build once again. It was always an exciting occasion, and I considered myself to be privileged when I witnessed one of the masters back at work.

Basil's trapping partner for over fifty years was Jocko Carle, a man who lived down the road from William. Jocko was the brother-in-law of

Mrs. Carle, the widow I stayed with for my first year on the reserve.

One day Basil suggested to Jocko that the two of them should build a birchbark canoe. Jocko was a skilled canoe maker of long standing, but he had not built a canoe for more than thirty years.

The last time Jocko had made a birchbark canoe was sometime during the Second World War. Equipped with a canvas canoe, he had gone trapping with a friend on the Coulonge River, sixty miles west of Maniwaki. In the spring, the rivers opened up quickly, but there was still much snow on the ground. They had a lot of gear, which included not only traps and furs but also meat from a moose they had just killed. Their canoe was overloaded.

While on his trapping rounds, Jocko had noticed a large birch tree, so they set about making a canoe. They boiled water to remove the bark from the tree, and used nails for the gunwales. To bind the ends and lash the thwarts into the gunwales, they used babiche from the moose they had just killed. In four days, they had a good fourteen-foot canoe. One man in each canoe, they made their way back to Maniwaki.

In the summer of 1979, Jocko and Basil retreated to Basil's trapping cabin on Rock Lake, sixty miles northwest of Maniwaki, and two weeks later came back with a birchbark canoe.

I had been spending some time in Ottawa and came back to see the finished canoe sitting in William's yard. This was the sort of alchemy for which I had been waiting: an Indian went into the woods with a crooked knife and an ax and came back with a birchbark canoe. It was as simple – and striking – as that. It was exciting to me to be in the presence of not one Indian builder of the birchbark canoe, but two.

Jocko knew William frequently sold birchbark canoes, but he did not know much more about it than that. He and Basil stayed in the woods as much as they could. Both guided in the summer and fall and trapped in the winter. Neither had a car or truck. Neither could read or write well. They avoided cities.

Jocko Carle and Basil Smith, River Désert Algonquin of Maniwaki, Quebec, at Round Lake, Quebec, 1981.

I spoke to Jocko about his canoe, and he told me he would like me to help him sell it. I called up the owner of an Indian crafts store in Ottawa, and she was in Maniwaki the next morning to buy the canoe.

Jocko had made many birchbark canoes with his father, brother, and sister throughout the 1930s. At that time, the going price was one dollar a foot. The family could sometimes turn out two or three canoes a week. To save labour, they used nails in the gunwales.

When I watched him work, it was obvious that Jocko's level of skill was outstanding. I think of him now sitting hour after hour carving ribs quickly and skillfully with his crooked knife, until all were finished and lying in a bundle.

Jocko liked beaver meat to such a degree that it amazed Basil. "When we're in the bush, Jocko gets a beaver in the trap and brings it

Birchbark canoe made by Jocko Carle and Basil Smith in 1979. This canoe was the first that Jocko had made for 37 years.

back to the camp. Then he skins it and puts the meat in the boiling water just as fast as he can. He takes it out of the water and starts eating it, and sometimes there's still blood on the meat!"

Jocko was one year older than Basil, and there was much affection between the two. Jocko weighed 220 pounds and Basil, on the occasion when I was able to get him on the scales, weighed 108 pounds. Basil would not have hurt a flea for the simple reason that it might have been a fairly even battle.

When I think of a capable white craftsperson who makes a good birchbark canoe, I think of a fellow hunkered over in great concentration, his intensity perhaps reflected in the sweat on his brow. I came to learn that the master Indian canoe builders were not like that. Their building of a canoe seems as natural as paddling one, and requires hardly more reflection.

Another difference I noticed was in how the Indians and whites display their skill.

I had known Jocko for three years before I learned that he was a birchbark canoe builder. Nicholas Jocko, another River Désert Algonquin, I had known for almost fifteen years and had spoken to often before I learned that he was a skilled birchbark canoe maker. With all the materials ready to hand, it used to take Nicholas ten days to make a full-size canoe. Occasionally he harvested bark with a birchbark torch in winter and spring. With his wife, Mary Louise, he made as many as five model canoes a day. Around 1952, they'd receive five dollars each for them.

◆

During a lull in the writing of the Commanda book, a friend from Maniwaki invited me to go on a canoe trip. He and some friends were going north to James Bay, an appendage of Hudson Bay. The trip would be only about a week long. Still, it might be an opportunity for me to try out a birchbark canoe on a long journey. Until this point, I had been in a birchbark canoe only a few times, for short tests with William.

I asked my friend if, of the three canoes we needed, I could take a birchbark canoe.

"Oh, gee," he said, somewhat worried. "Do you think that would be very fast?" We did have to make a trip of over a week, after all.

"No, not really; I think a bush plane would be much faster," I replied. I found the lack of confidence in the birchbark canoe discouraging at times, especially when it came from an avid canoeist.

Years before, when I was working in the lumber camp at Ottawa Lake and making toy birchbark canoes to pass the time, I had often reflected that it was too bad birchbark canoes could not be made and used still. Why not make a full-size birchbark canoe and cover it with fibreglass so it would last? From my new perspective, I knew this was a silly misconception of the birchbark canoe, but it reflected the ideas most uninitiated people had about them.

I was not alone in my bizarre misconceptions. Writers of general interest and historical books nearly always referred to birchbark canoes as being fragile. A canvas canoe expert said that birchbark canoes "couldn't hold any weight." Yet later, I put seven hundred pounds of stones in an eleven-foot canoe I made with Basil Smith before the water level rose to the bottom edge of the gunwales.

Nevertheless, I felt I owed it to the others in the party to do some preliminary tests in a birchbark canoe before making the long trip. First my friend and I went twelve miles down the Désert River in canvas canoes at a leisurely pace that brought us to town in four hours. We repeated the trip a few days later in the birchbark canoe that Jocko and Basil had made. That trip took only ten minutes longer, which convinced me to take the birchbark canoe on the James Bay trip.

I bought the canoe from Jocko and Basil. The bark was quite thick, stronger than any Jocko and William could remember seeing, but it made for a heavy canoe. It was sixteen feet long and weighed eighty-five pounds.

My canoe mate was Peter Lemieux from Ottawa. I found out later that his grandfather, a man accustomed to the woods, was quite nervous about Peter making the trip in the birchbark canoe. Apparently he would have been more confident had Peter been in another sort of canoe.

I entered the project with abandon. Like many of the old Indian canoeists, I could not swim. Peter, though, was an avid whitewater canoeist, much more experienced than I was. Since he had also worked as a lifeguard, he was a good man to have in the bow. The fact that the leader of the party was an experienced skindiver convinced me I was covered for any eventuality.

We began the trip along the Abitibi River near Fraserdale, Ontario, about fifteen miles from Moosonee, a part Cree town close to James Bay. Our birchbark canoe was fully loaded and balanced, but it proved to be too buoyant, even with our gear weighing perhaps one hundred pounds. The canoe floated so high in the water that the wind caught us from the side and began to turn us around. The two canvas canoes had as much dunnage as we had but a fair amount less freeboard. They were low in the water, each with about five inches of freeboard; we had nine.

A difference in speed became apparent on the first day. We were the slowest of the three. On long stretches, the canoes were strung out and we were normally third in line. Our consolation lay in the fact that there was as much difference between the first and second canoe as there was between the second canoe and us.

Our first two days and nights were on a broad river, so our birchbark canoe did not meet any real tests. When the first rapids loomed ahead, two of the men went before us in a canvas canoe to reconnoitre. They came back with a scratch on their canoe bottom that went into the canvas, and they reported the rapids were bad — bad in our terms, since a hole in our canoe could have been trouble.

I was more than a little concerned about my own performance in rapids, since I had little experience with them. But we decided to try it.

The others went ahead to find channels through the rocks. We saw the two canoes smashing into rocks, and we hit hard in the same area. We jumped out of the canoe to guide it through the rocks.

"Watch it, Peter!" I yelled because of some dangerous-looking rocks that were coming up.

Although ours was the heaviest canoe, the fact that it was floating high gave us an advantage over our travelling companions.

The other canoes were bouncing on the rocks and the men spent as much time out of their canoes as we did. I was most afraid not of damaging the canoe while we were in it, but of it being wrested from us, filled with water, and smashed to pieces. We were continually fighting the current.

We had to wrestle these rapids for the next three miles. The canoes hit rocks all the time. Water was in all the canoes, a lot of it brought in when we jumped back into them. It was impossible to tell if any of the canoes were leaking.

When finally we left the long stretch of rapids and came to a wide part of the river, we went to the bank, turned our canoes over, and inspected them for damage.

Our canoe was scraped only superficially; no water would pass through the bottom. One of the canvas canoes had taken a hard scrape, but it did not look as if it would leak. The second canvas canoe had taken the most damage. Rocks had made deep scratches in several places. One of the spots had to be patched with strong duct tape.

Our journey ended several days later with rapids not quite as bad as that first set.

The trip in the birchbark canoe was a revelation. It confirmed what I had hoped about the birchbark canoe: that it is no more fragile than most other canoes. Of the three canoes we had on our trip, it was the only one that did not require some repair during the course of the trip. Jocko Carle and Basil Smith had built the canoe without ever having tested the gumming job in the water. Nevertheless, it did not take on a drop of water through the hull during the week-long trip.

CHAPTER 11

Although helping to build a birchbark canoe the previous summer had been exciting, the best adventure was yet to come: building a birchbark canoe on my own. I decided that I did not want to work on a building platform as William did. I wanted to build my canoe on the ground as Jocko did. Nor did I want interruptions.

Turtle Lake was a wilderness lake about three miles long, fifteen miles west of Maniwaki. There was a beach on the north end of the lake at a little bay that would be ideal for building a canoe and for camping.

Jocko gave me a roll of birchbark. William lent me a few tools. Hans Andersen lent a standup tent, my pup tent not being appropriate for a long stay. I also collected the other materials for the canoe and as many supplies as I thought I would need while in the bush.

I hired a truck to take me to Turtle Lake. There, I set up the roomy tent and cached my food to prevent mice and raccoons from getting into it. I put the roll of bark in the water to soak. It was the first of August.

My basic resource was the teaching I had received from Jocko and William. Another was the old standby, Edwin Tappan Adney's *Bark Canoes and Skin Boats of North America*. I also found myself in the unusual position of consulting the birchbark canoe section of my own book, the one I had written about William and Mary Commanda. In addition to these books I had Robert Ritzenthaler's *Building a Chippewa Indian Birchbark Canoe*, published by the Milwaukee Public Museum, and *The Weymontaching Birchbark Canoe* by Camil Guy, published by the National Museum of Man. I never knew which of these books would contain a bit of information that would set me straight on a particular issue.

I had set a tentative timetable: perhaps two days to split and carve the ribs and about the same amount of time to prepare the sheathing and spruce root. After working out the time required for other operations, I came up with a projected completion date about two weeks away. Was I dreaming!

True, Jocko and Basil made a canoe in five days. William took much longer, but I thought I would be on the job more than he.

Each stage I had calculated in the building process was drawn out – sometimes drastically. It was easy – and fun – to split the spruce root in the warm sun. As I worked, I watched the loons almost running along the surface of the water for a couple of hundred yards trying to take off. I took breaks to swim off a point a short distance away. When I got thirsty, I waded into the lake to take a drink; other times I had the teapot on the fire. It was so idyllic that I thought I had died and gone to birchbark canoe makers' heaven.

I had not worked much with a crooked knife while apprenticing with William, but, taking a cue from Jocko, I was making my first canoe entirely with a crooked knife. The drawknife I had left in Maniwaki. My hand ached every evening – the crooked knife is almost like a one-handed drawknife, which means that the leverage on the blade must be maintained with the wrist.

Though making the ribs went well, it took twice as long as I had planned. The thwarts were really difficult. I made them out of white birch that I cut near my campsite. The grain was somewhat twisty, which meant that I was hacking away at the thwarts much longer than I should have been. It was one of a number of glaring problems that would not be too difficult to remedy the next time I made a canoe.

It turned out I had harvested only slightly more cedar than I needed for gunwales. There was the inwale, outwale, and gunwale cap on each side to make. That meant that I did not dare make a mistake. I sweated as I split the gunwales, using a fork at the base of a tree for a fulcrum.

I had one great advantage at the campsite on Turtle Lake – a birch-bark canoe. A few months earlier, a friend had told me of an advertisement in the town newspaper for a birchbark canoe on sale for forty dollars. It turned out to be a very nice Maniwaki canoe from perhaps the 1930s, so I bought it. It was fourteen feet long, a very common length for that time, and had very nice lines. Through lack of proper care over the years it had sustained some damage, but it was still a good canoe to use as a pattern. I had given it to an Indian boy on the reserve, and he lent it to me for my special project.

When Jocko gave me the roll of birchbark, he warned that it was not a prime roll. He explained that it was probably not such a good idea to use excellent birchbark for a first canoe, since, in all likelihood, the first one was not going to be a very good one.

As I worked, I began to see that Jocko had not underestimated the quality of his gift. Wading in the water one day for a drink, I decided to check the soaking bark. Some of the eyes opened up as I pushed down on the bark with my thumb. Every one of those eyes would be a leak in the finished canoe. I learned then, and it was confirmed for me over and over again in later years, that in a birchbark canoe, the bark is everything. Too many things can go wrong if the bark is bad. While an excellent sheet of birchbark will not be an excellent canoe if the builder is mediocre, good workmanship by a good builder loses much if the bark is bad.

William came out to visit when I was a week into the project. He simply observed. I knew he was curious. In the early stages, however, it is almost impossible to tell how the project will turn out. William's curiosity was therefore not completely satisfied, but we enjoyed a cup of tea and a visit. It started raining while we visited, and he helped me lash a tarp over the canoe-building bed.

Other friends also came out to check on my progress. A friend came one night, and late in the evening while we were having a couple of beers by the fire, a moose swam a hundred yards in front of the campsite. Turtle Lake was almost like a dream.

In time, I had carved all the wooden components for the canoe and was ready to put up the sides and start lashing the gunwales with spruce root.

Lashing the gunwales gave form to the canoe and gave me a feeling of progress. The canoe lines were still fairly good, although I had a hard time conceptualizing the top line and the bottom line, called the sheer and the rocker. Knowing what they should look like was easy; I had the other birchbark canoe right there. Achieving it was something else again. Those two lines, in fact, would turn out to be the basic shortcoming of the finished canoe.

I made a trip back home for supplies. Jocko was working on a canoe in his back yard. My project was looking like an all-month affair. "*Ki gi ickwa tcîmanike na?*" he asked. "*Wîbätc gata sôkipo!* Did you finish your canoe? It's going to snow soon!"

"It's coming; it's coming," I replied.

The day arrived when it was time to bend the ribs. A lot of things can happen when making a birchbark canoe. Most of these things, I found, are bad. Rib-bending day is perhaps the most tense period in the building process. Jocko made rather thick ribs for his canoes; he once broke twenty-two ribs in the process of trying to bend forty good ones. Several broken ribs could send me back to the crooked knife for an extra day's work, and it might entail harvesting more cedar. The bending, however, went well; I only broke a few ribs. The next job was to put the binder in the canoe. A series of struts, the binder forces apart two long battens at the bottom of the canoe so that the ribs dry in the form of the bottom of the canoe. When I put my canoe in the sun to dry, I noticed that the ribs were not forced down enough with the binder. The bark came a couple of inches below the ribs, leaving a space. I was able to remedy that later by forcing the ribs down when they were permanently inserted in the canoe.

William paid me another visit. The canoe drying in the sun, although not yet finished, made quite a different impression. I had taken care to lash the gunwales neatly with the spruce root. The ribs were even and smooth, and though they were a couple of inches off the bottom, it was possible that the finished canoe would be quite acceptable.

I considered my birchbark canoe building sort of an Indian test of manhood. Of course, I hadn't passed my white test of manhood yet (being in a forty-hour-a-week salaried job for ten years, and having a back strong enough to support a crushing mortgage).

Some people are dismissive of young Indians who do not show interest in Indian skills, such as birchbark canoe making. Few of them nowadays do. My father was a good hunter and butcher and knew automobile mechanics. I am deficient in all three areas. My grandfather spoke Swedish as his first language. I did not know a word of the language until a few years ago.

◆

Sometimes I had trouble sleeping, I think, because the canoe was on my mind. Using reading as a soporific, I'd reach for a candle in the tent, light it, and open a book for a while before drifting off to sleep.

I had baked beans in the sand by first making a good hardwood fire and then burying the bean pot under the coals. There they baked slowly overnight, and in the morning they were warm and ready to eat.

I got up the next morning to eat a plate or two of beans, drink some coffee, and contemplate my last major task – inserting the ribs in the canoe for their final placement. In this operation, all the rib ends had to be cut off quite precisely. The sheathing would then be carefully placed to cover the entire inside of the canoe, forcing the ribs into the canoe under great pressure. The two ends of the ribs were bevelled and fitted into a bevel on the outboard side of the inwale, where the bark sheet was sandwiched between the inwale and the outwale. The ribs were hammered in with a mallet. The pressure created by the ribs was so intense that the ribs could not all be placed vertically at first. They were left slightly short of vertical until the bark sheet adjusted to the pressure. To help it adjust to the ribs, the bark was wetted. A few hours later, the ribs were pounded to the vertical.

I calculated that I had only to place some already prepared sheathing in the canoe and cut off the ends of about forty ribs and I would be almost finished my canoe. I hoped this would be in time for lunch, maybe by one o'clock at the latest. Then I would have all afternoon and evening to putter around with the little things.

Such are the plans of first-timers. First of all, the sheathing had to cover the entire inside of the hull, meaning that the pieces of sheathing had to go up to the gunwales. It was a job that took four hands. These pieces kept falling down and I finally resorted to taping them up temporarily to keep them in place. Pressure on the sheathing caused a strake to break, and it had to be replaced. It became clear that the rib was too long, so out it came. I trimmed another quarter of an inch off each side with the crooked knife. That wasn't enough, so it came out again and another quarter of an inch came off. A quarter of an inch too much and the rib would be too loose in the finished canoe.

So it went. Lunchtime passed and then some, and the first thing I knew it was nine o'clock in the evening and I had two candles lit in the canoe so that I could see to finish this important part of the job before I went to bed. And I had hoped to finish by lunch.

The two jobs that remained were rather minor ones: the two gunwale caps had to be pegged onto the gunwales, and then the whole canoe had to be gummed. Although they were also jobs for which four hands would be useful, it was not hard to get this work done. I was about twenty-four hours behind my original plan when I took the canoe for a test trip.

Grabbing a paddle, I stepped in and went toward the south end of the lake three miles distant. Although there were a number of things to improve on the next time, I was happy with my first canoe.

It paddled like a leaf, as most birchbark canoes do. The thirteen-foot craft was so buoyant it would have been good to have fifty pounds of ballast in the bow. Some of the eyes had opened up, so there was a little water in the bottom.

I paddled down to the distant bay where I went ashore for a few minutes before turning around to come back.

On my return trip, I spotted a squirrel swimming in the water. I slowed down to watch him and thought he was going to cross behind me. Instead, he turned and swam straight for the canoe. He climbed up the spruce root lacing on the stern and ran quickly past me along the gunwale cap to perch on the bow looking back at me. I let him stay there a while, and he seemed quite content. Then I headed to the nearby shore, thinking I had better let him off.

When we landed, I quietly walked away so that the squirrel could jump off. But he didn't want to go, so after a short time I got back in the canoe and paddled off to my camp, the squirrel still perched on the stem-head of the bow, looking at me.

Overhead a red-tailed hawk swooped shouting, "Keeer! keeer!" and the squirrel looked up.

I pulled up to my camp and the squirrel jumped to the beach and ran off. It was with some excitement that I pulled the canoe up onto the sand. The thrill was not because I had just made a pleasant little canoe trip, but because I had made the canoe.

A friend with a truck took me, the canoe, and my gear back to Maniwaki. My two- or three-week schedule had turned into a thirty-two-day endeavour.

Naturally I was anxious to see the reactions of friends. Hans Andersen took one look at the canoe and shook my hand. I was eager for Jocko's opinion. He had helped me with some of the refinements of birchbark canoe construction and I admired his canoes.

He examined the canoe and then looked at me. "That's a damn good canoe for a first one."

Two axes are used to score a straight line along the entire length of the trunk of the tree. The line must go down through the bark into the cambium layer, so that all the layers of bark come off and the sheet of bark remains whole. The bark is peeled back carefully from the score.

Jim peels a sixteen-foot sheet of bark from a white birch tree. Good quality bark usually peels better than bad quality bark.

Jim has three large rolls of birchbark across the gunwales of his canoe. The two rolls closest to him are each big enough to make a sixteen-foot canoe.

Jim Jerome and his son Corey saw down a large cedar tree. Jim has tested the tree for a straight grain by pulling a strip of bark up the trunk. If the strip goes around the tree, the grain is twisted and the bark unsuitable for canoe building

Jim splits a long, straight cedar log for gunwale stock. The log is first split in half, then in quarters. The punk wood in the centre of the log will be taken out later.

Using the table leg as a fulcrum, Jim splits the inwales of the canoe. Because he has already carved the long piece of cedar with his crooked knife, so the inwales are nearly finished.

Jim bends the stem-piece over his knee. He has already split the stem-piece six times to the middle of the batten, and has soaked the stem-piece for several days.

To maintain the curvature while the stem-piece dries, it is tied to form a precise profile.

At Round Lake, Quebec, in 1981, Jocko Carle carves a rib with a crooked knife. The shavings are all from the work on one birchbark canoe. In the background, the canoe is starting to take shape. The bottom shape of the canoe is created by a building frame (no visible in photo) that is weighted down with rocks. The bark sides have been raised and are held in place by vertical stakes.

Jim Jerome, at his camp on Rapid Lake, carves a piece of sheathing with his crooked knife. The already thin sheathing has to be backed up with a board so that it will not break while it is being carved thinner.

Jim takes great care to centre the building frame (which forms the bottom shape of the canoe) on the bark sheet. Next he will put rocks on the frame and raise the bark to form the sides of the canoe.

Jim Jerome splits sheathing and Angèle Jerome sews moccasins at Rapid Lake, Quebec, in 1985.

At Jim's canoe building camp at Rapid Lake, gunwale stock lies on the bank and finished gunwales soak in the water.

At Round Lake, Quebec, in 1981, Jocko Carle stakes up the ends of the main sheet of bark to begin to form the bow of the canoe.

Ernestine Gidmark and Jim Jerome examine the bow of a canoe for straightness. Inner and outer stakes clamp the inwales and outwales together. The gunwales are almost ready for lashing with spruce root.

Basil Smith, at Round Lake, Quebec, in 1981, has just sewn the side piece of bark to the main sheet.

Jim Jerome uses both hands to cut the thick bark down to gunwale level; he will lash it with spruce root next. The centre thwart of yellow birch has been mortised into the gunwales but not yet lashed to them.

Angèle Jerome lashes the gunwales (now a "sandwich" of inwale, bark, and outwale) with roots of the white spruce tree. One of these lashings binds the thwart to the gunwale. The rocks and building frame are still in the canoe.

Jocko Carle puts pieces of sheathing temporarily in the bottom of the canoe, just prior to bending the ribs. Ribs and other pieces of sheathing are on the table in the background. The five thwarts of white birch are permanently lashed to the gunwales. Cross braces are nailed to the gunwales temporarily so that the canoe does not splay when the ribs are left to dry.

Jocko Carle bends ribs before sunrise at Round Lake, Quebec, in 1981.

Jim Jerome lays ribs across the gunwales of the canoe in order to measure the ribs for proper bending. On each rib, a line is drawn three finger-lengths from the inwale on each side of the canoe.

Jocko Carle bends the ribs. He must force them quite snugly against the bottom of the canoe so that they take on the proper curvature of the hull.

At Jim Jerome's canoe building camp, the almost finished canoe is on the building bed. Over the fire are a frying pan for baking bannock and a bucket for boiling spruce root. Gunwale caps are steaming in the diagonal tube, the bottom end of which is in the fire.

Jim Jerome's completed canoe is now in the collection of the Canadian Canoe Museum.

CHAPTER 12

My next experience with birchbark canoes was guided by Jocko Carle. I had written the book, *The Indian Crafts of William and Mary Commanda*, for McGraw-Hill Ryerson, and I wanted to record as much existing information about the Algonquin builders as I could while they were still living.

Jocko Carle lived only a few doors down from William, and he occasionally made a canoe behind his house. I visited him often. Unfailingly kind, Jocko described the fine points of birchbark canoe making, but the student had to remain alert, for there was often a tease inserted somewhere in Jocko's instruction.

Once I came up to Jocko in the back yard as he was just finishing a canoe. He was making animal designs in the winter bark, the bark taken off the trees in the spring and fall. At that time of year, the cold leaves a dark layer into which the design can be scraped.

I stood by him watching silently. Suddenly he stopped while drawing the moose. He seemed unable to go on. Then he looked at me and asked perplexedly, "Does a moose have a tail?"

Birchbark canoes with bark decoration.

Jocko made an excellent canoe, so I wanted to record his method next. I contacted the National Museum of Man and was given a grant to record the birchbark canoe building process of Jocko Carle.

In the month of August 1981, we went to Round Lake, about forty miles northwest of Maniwaki, where there was a small cabin. Basil had been there for several weeks before Jocko and I arrived. We settled in with our gear and began the project.

◆

Jocko was one of sixteen children of John Carle of Petawagama Lake, about eighty miles north of Maniwaki. John Carle was a well-known canoe maker. He died at the age of 105 only a few years before I met Jocko.

Of all the boys in the family, only Jocko and his brother Peter were canoe builders. The others moved away for work. Jocko started building some canoes on his own in the late 1920s, working with some combination of his father, Peter, and his sister. At that time, the family moved down to the reserve in Maniwaki, and in season they often made two or three canoes per week. In those days, good bark could be obtained readily on the reserve.

Other Indian families came down from the bush around the same time to live on the Maniwaki reserve. The move often coincided with their adoption of more advanced tools. The Carles made the change from using a bone awl (*mîkos*) to using a steel awl. Mary Commanda came with her family from the upper Gatineau River area. Until the move, she had often used sinew ("Indian thread") for sewing.

The Round Lake area was a good source for most of the raw materials needed for the canoe. Basil scouted out a good birch only a hundred yards behind the cabin. To get the bark, we simply grabbed our axes, chainsaw, and ropes and walked back to the tree. We cut cedar on the eastern shore of the lake about a mile from the cabin, and found our spruce root in a clearing along a bush road about ten miles from Round Lake.

Jocko had high standards. He tested the bark by making an ax cut about six feet up from the base of the tree. Tearing off a small piece of bark, he bent it back on itself to make sure that it was pliable enough to resist cracking. He also checked to see that it did not split into layers. Jocko explained that occasionally bark could be too thin on the bottom of the tree and of sufficient thickness on the top, or vice versa, and that this had to be kept in mind when getting bark.

This tree proved to be all right. The trunk was straight and the bark of good quality. The tree even leaned in the right direction, meaning it would be easy to fell at the desired spot.

As Jocko began to clear brush from around the trunk, Basil cut

Removing a sheet of bark to be used for the side piece.

small trees that would be placed under the falling birch trunk to form a protective bed. Jocko cleared out the area where the tree would land. Then all of a sudden, as he was finishing his clearing task, he began jumping up and down and quickly hopped over to one side. Indians have been known to chant or pray at certain stages during the canoe-building process, but I had never seen Indians gathering bark perform what could have been described as a chant or a dance. Perhaps Jocko, knowing this was an important project being done for the museum, had decided to return to traditional methods throughout the process. I, in my unaccustomed role as ethnographer, thought that if Jocko was going to do a little ceremonial dance it should certainly not go unrecorded.

I dropped the ax and quickly ran for my notebook. It was only when I picked it up and turned around that I realized that Jocko had stepped into a bees' nest.

Finally we cut the tree and removed the bark. Back at the lake, Jocko put the bark roll in the water to soak. He said that good bark could be stored dry almost indefinitely and then made usable simply by resoaking it.

Basil, quite content in the warm August shade with the breezes blowing in from Round Lake, prepared the spruce root. Then it came time for him to go down near the lake and prepare the building bed for the canoe. He chose a shaded, sandy spot near the lake. When the spot was nearly ready, he walked briskly to where Jocko was working and relayed some bad news. One of the bushes at the edge of the site harboured yet another bees' nest, and Basil had just aroused them inadvertently.

"Maybe we should go into the honey business," Jocko said.

We soon established a routine. Jocko would get up before sunrise and start a fire in the stove, then go down to the canoe-building site and build a fire there, or simply start working if no fire was needed that day.

Unrolling the bark on the building bed.

When Basil had breakfast ready, we would all eat and then go down to work.

At lunch, Jocko would call over to Basil with great affection, "Heh, Basil! *Kiga wîsinimin na?* Heh, Basil? Are we going to eat?"

Basil would drop whatever he was working on and slowly walk off to the cabin, humming to himself. After fifteen minutes or so, Jocko would set the crooked knife down and go up to the cabin to eat. The same routine would be repeated for supper.

Invariably, just after sunset, I would say to Jocko, "Say, don't you think you ought to call it a day?" As if just then noticing that it was getting dark, he'd look up, put his crooked knife down, and come in. We would all be in bed by nine o'clock.

Splitting ribs. The blank has been carved previously so that splitting it produces two virtually finished ribs.

After lunch the first day, I fetched the roll of birchbark from the lake. We unrolled the bark on the building bed, a process I had seen often but that still held a fascination now as I worked with these two gentle men in peace far in the woods. We then placed the building frame on the bark and loaded it with heavy rocks. Jocko next positioned the gunwale frame at the proper height, clamping the gunwales to it. Basil and I began the long job of lashing the gunwales with spruce root while Jocko finished carving some ribs. He was so fast with his crooked knife that he sometimes seemed to bury himself in the shavings.

"*Ki da anibiciwaboke,*" Jocko said after a while. This time I got up to make tea for the three of us.

After the gunwales were lashed — a long job — Jocko and Basil

Pounding the ribs into the canoe.

mortised the thwarts into the gunwale and then lashed them with spruce root.

Finally it was time to bend the ribs. We removed the rocks and the frame from the canoe, and Basil swept out the bottom. Water was boiling. Jocko took a pair of ribs from the bunch that had been in the lake and ladled boiling water over them for a few minutes. He then sat down on a bench to bend the ribs.

As soon as the ribs were bent, he carried them to the canoe. "Come on, Basil!" he called, and Basil walked over with a hammer and nails. Jocko stepped into the canoe with the pair of ribs and forced them, one on top of the other, into place on the bottom. Then he took the top rib and moved it along to the next position nearer the bow. As soon as a rib was forced down as far as it would go, Basil put a nail through each end of it and into the gunwale. The nails were only temporary, but held the ribs in place until they could dry. When the ribs were all bent and in place, Jocko and Basil put a binder in the bottom of the canoe to force the ribs to maintain their proper shape. The struts and the bent ribs themselves exerted a lot of pressure on the gunwales.

Two years earlier, when Jocko had resumed building birchbark canoes, he and Basil had gone to Rock Lake to build one. During this project, Jocko had forgotten a minor detail.

After the binder has been put in the canoe, cross braces must be fixed to the gunwales in such a way as to keep them together. On Rock Lake, he had neglected to use such cross braces. After Jocko and Basil had bent the ribs and positioned them in the canoe to dry, they woke up the next morning to find the canoe spread wide, the lashing of the thwarts ripped and the gunwales wide open.

As we reached this point in the process, Jocko's inclination to keep moving would not let him rest. Even as the canoe dried in the sun, he started to scrape animal designs on the bark.

On the last day of construction, Jocko and Basil cut the tops of the ribs to the proper level and fitted them in the canoe over the sheathing.

To gum the canoe, Jocko used pine rosin, which had a dark hue. To increase the rosin's viscosity, he had only to add lard little by little until he was sure that the mixture was of the proper consistency. Jocko left no doubt as to how he was able to judge the delicate balance that would be an effective mixture of rosin and lard. "Experience," he said.

Using a wooden spatula, Jocko applied the gum to all the seams, covering the unsewn gores along the sides and the sewn seam where the extra piece of bark had been added along the side. He put the gum directly on the sewing on the ends of the canoe without adding any strip of fabric or other material over it, as was done sometimes on Algonquin canoes. When the gum had to be worked into place, Jocko and Basil wet their thumbs so that the gum would not stick when they pressed it.

When all was ready, we carried the canoe down to the lake for a try and for some pictures. Jocko and Basil were satisfied with the canoe, and it did not require any further gumming.

Another man from the reserve in Maniwaki came to pick us up with a truck. We played a little with the canoe, and all three of them got into it while I took a few pictures. Basil was in the bow, Jocko paddled in the stern, and the friend sat in the middle. With 530 pounds in the canoe, there were still three or four inches of freeboard.

Back on shore, Jocko turned the canoe upside down on the carpenter's horses and looked over the hull until he was satisfied that everything was all right.

There was one question I wanted to ask for the record. I was admiring the rib work and the resiliency of the bark when I inquired of Jocko how long the canoe would last.

He looked at me and, as if answering a hint of incredulity in the question, responded in a suitably explicit way: "Forever!"

The canoe that Jocko and Basil built that summer on Round Lake is now part of the collection of the National Museums of Canada. The grant that I received from the National Museum of Man to record the project was part of a program to do what they called urgent ethnology. The need for the program was only too evident.

Jocko Carle died four months after he completed the birchbark canoe on Round Lake.

The funeral cortège on the reserve in Maniwaki was a clear testimony to the respect people had for Jocko. The procession stretched from the Indian church to the bridge on Bitobi Road, a distance of more than half a mile.

Jocko's widow gave his crooked knife to Basil. Basil said to me, "He was my friend. He was always ready to go in the bush."

CHAPTER 13

Henry David Thoreau had a strong interest in the birchbark canoe. His travel narrative, *The Maine Woods*, was actually intended to be, in part, a practical guide for campers. The book is a wilderness adventure illustrating the wild side of Thoreau's world.

I admired innumerable things about Thoreau but one with which I most empathized, and most wanted to emulate, was his idea that people could best flourish by living on the borderline, literally, between civilization and wilderness, thereby deriving the greatest benefits from each.

My lifestyle evolved into a simpler one: I lived beside a lake with no name in a cabin sixteen by twenty feet, furnished with a double bed for myself and another for guests. I had no electrical or telephone bills and only a modest propane bill. With wood available for the cutting and the opportunity to have a garden and to hunt and fish if I wanted, expenditures were minimal.

Many people in modern society think that the easiest way to cure any bad development or malady that besets them – or to celebrate something – is to spoil themselves. Usually this inclination is manifested in the acquisition of some dispensable material thing, or in consuming more food, often beyond what is needed.

The modern man "works" hard all day, comes home, and plops in front of the television for hours in the evening because he doesn't have the energy to undertake proper exercise. Perhaps the reason is the reverse: he lacks energy because he does not have proper exercise.

Where does all this devotion to materialism and this lack of exercise lead? Well, it leads to the malady of the twentieth century — stress. Stress kills. And the increase in materialism in North America (just since the 1960s!) is a big part of it. In the evolutionary sense, we are not meant to do certain of the things we do. We have been three million years in the forest, three thousand years on the farm, but only three hundred years in the factory. We have been living the life of modern technology for only the last fifty years.

The first trip Thoreau describes in *The Maine Woods* is a voyage he made down the Chesuncook River in Maine in 1853 when he was thirty-six years old. His Indian guide was Joe Aitteon, a man of unmixed Indian blood who was twenty-four.

A steamer carried Thoreau and Aitteon part way up the river to begin their trip. Along the way, they passed two timber cruisers that had "a fine new birch on board, larger than ours." Apparently it was common long ago, from Maine to Minnesota, to refer to a birchbark canoe as a "birch." Throughout the book, when Thoreau refers to the white birch tree, he most often calls it "canoe birch."

At their first camp, Thoreau recounts their settling in for the night:

We now proceeded to get dinner, which always turned out to be tea, and to pitch canoes, for which purpose a large iron pot lay permanently on the bank. This we did in company with the explorers. Both Indians and whites use a mixture of rosin and grease for this purpose — that is, for pitching, not the dinner.

Joe took a small brand from the fire, and blowed the heat and flame against the pitch on his birch, and so melted and spread it. Sometimes he put his mouth over the place and sucked, to see if it admitted air, and at one place, where we stopped, he placed his canoe high on crossed stakes, and poured water into it.

Their birchbark canoe was nineteen and a half feet long, two and a half feet in the beam, and fourteen inches deep. The ends were virtually identical. The canoe was painted green; Aitteon thought that this adversely affected the gum job. There were three of them in the canoe, for a total weight of nearly six hundred pounds. They had two rock maple paddles and one of bird's-eye maple. Aitteon placed birchbark on the bottom for them to sit on, and what Thoreau called "slanted cedar splints" against the thwarts to protect their backs. Their guide sat on the thwart in the stern.

Aitteon peeled a piece of canoe birch for a moose call, which Thoreau calls a "hunting horn." Thoreau says that the canoe was pitched whenever they stopped long enough to build a fire.

Thoreau especially enjoyed camping at night. He lay awake watching sparks from the fire shooting fifty feet into the night sky. He says they were as interesting as fireworks. "We do not suspect how much our chimneys have concealed."

Aitteon paddled on one side only, using the gunwale as a fulcrum. Thoreau asked him how the ribs were fastened to the gunwales. Since Aitteon said that he did not know, apparently he was not a canoe maker himself. It is strange that they did not look on the underside of the gunwale to find out the answer to their question.

They saw Indians of Aitteon's acquaintance making canoes on the Caucomgomoc River.

Thoreau comments on who went into the woods in those days: "For one that comes with a pencil to sketch or sing, a thousand come with an ax or rifle." While paddling with Aitteon, he observes that ". . . our life should be lived as tenderly and daintily as one would pick a flower."

An annoying aspect of the book is Thoreau's rendering of Aitteon's "Indian talk." He has Aitteon saying things such as "Me sure get some moose." After I had spent so much time studying and appreciating the Indian language, this device of Thoreau's grated on my ear very much. It is a rather insensitive portrayal that one would not have expected of Thoreau. In fact, later in the book, he not only refers to his own study of the Indian language, but also makes it obvious that he has a growing respect for it:

> There can be no more startling evidence of their being a distinct and comparatively aboriginal race, than to hear this unaltered Indian language, which the white man cannot speak or understand.

The language fascinated him, though he understood not a syllable:

> I felt as though I stood, or rather lay [he was in his bedroll by the fire], as near to the primitive man of America, that night, as any of its discoverers ever did.

They came upon an Indian carving a thwart with a crooked knife, which Thoreau called a

> singularly shaped knife, such as I have since seen other Indians using. The blade was thin, about three-quarters of an inch wide, and eight or nine inches long, but curved out of its plane into a hook, which he said is more convenient to shave with. As the Indians very far north and northwest use the same kind of knife, I suspect it was made according to an aboriginal pattern, though some white artisans may use a similar one.

And then Thoreau makes a confession that shows how smitten he was with the birchbark canoe, and illustrates how enamoured of the craft others became, including, only a little more than thirty years later, Edwin Tappan Adney, when they saw a birchbark canoe being built, a process that is truly alchemy:

> I made a faithful study of canoe-building, and I thought that I should like to serve an apprenticeship of that trade for one season, going into the woods with my "boss," making the canoe there, and returning in it at last.

Thoreau's next trip was on the Allagash and the east branch of the Penobscot River. His guide this time was a birchbark canoe maker named Joe Polis from Old Town, Maine.

When Thoreau came upon Polis, the guide was scraping a deer hide on a scraping log on Indian Island, near Old Town. Polis had brought their canoe by train to Bangor, from where he had to carry it three-quarters of a mile on his shoulders. Thoreau, jovial but perhaps a little thoughtless, tried to break the ice with Polis while the latter was huffing and puffing under the heavy canoe.

The canoe was put on top of a stage. Apparently the driver was used to transporting canoes; he put bits of carpeting under the canoe to prevent chafing.

The canoe trip itself started on Moosehead Lake. Their table the first night was a large sheet of birchbark that Polis laid on the ground tawny side up.

Thoreau's guide was always very careful in approaching the shore in the canoe, as he was worried about damaging it on the rocks. Nor did Polis want anyone to step into the canoe near the shore when the canoe was not floating. At night when they made camp, Polis laid a log over the upturned canoe so that it would not blow away in a high wind.

The trip did not keep Thoreau from philosophizing, of course. "I have much to learn of the Indian," he said, "nothing of the missionary. I am not sure but all that would tempt me to teach the Indian my religion would be his promise to teach me *his*."

Polis and Thoreau at one point met a St. Francis Indian engaged in canoe building, whereupon a discussion ensued about the best spruce root to use in building a birchbark canoe. Polis thought that black spruce was best; the other Indian claimed that white spruce was. According to Polis, white spruce roots broke easily and were hard to split, and also were hard to get because they grew deep in the ground, but the black spruce roots were near the surface and were tougher.

Thoreau thought he could make a birchbark canoe, but Polis expressed great doubt when he heard this.

Together they prepared some spruce root. Polis grubbed at the ground, distinguishing the black spruce root from other roots. He split the root evenly, but when Thoreau tried to do this himself, the split was uneven. Polis had contracted the sewing of the canoe to be done for fifty cents, though he did all the rest. (About 130 years later, Jocko Carle paid his son one hundred dollars for the same root work, while Jim Jerome of Rapid Lake paid Lina Nottaway twenty dollars.)

◆

The great lyrical depiction of the birchbark canoe in literature occurs, of course, in *The Song of Hiawatha*, a narrative poem by Henry Wadsworth Longfellow.

It was published in 1855 when Longfellow was forty-eight. In his diary of the summer before, he says that his object was to weave Indian traditions together to form a whole. What he lacked in ethnology, he made up for in poetic interpretation. The traditions upon which he formulated his poem are basically Ojibway, but the character of Hiawatha was modelled upon an Iroquois national hero.

The idea for the poem came to Longfellow from the Finnish epic, the *Kalevala* – the word is the poetic name for Finland – a compilation of ballads and lyrical songs memorized and handed down by bards and common folk in Finland for generations. He borrowed the metre for *The Song of Hiawatha* from a German translation of the *Kalevala*.

The ethnology for his epic poem Longfellow took from *Algic Researches* by Henry Rowe Schoolcraft. He was agent to the Indians of the Lake Superior region and was married to an Ojibway woman. As superintendent of Indian affairs for Michigan, Schoolcraft supervised an 1836 treaty by which the Ojibway ceded much of the northern part of the state. Hiawatha wouldn't have liked that. In Longfellow's epic, Hiawatha is an Indian nationalist trying to unite all Indians – Pawnee, Blackfoot, Delaware, Mohawk, and so on.

The poem is often weak on ethnology and philology, but in its poetic descriptions of the birchbark canoe it will probably never be surpassed:

> Give me of your bark, O Birch-Tree
> Of your yellow bark, O Birch-Tree!
> Growing by the rushing river,
> Tall and stately in the valley!
> I a light canoe will build me,
> Build a swift Cheemaun for sailing,
> That shall float upon the river.
> Like a yellow leaf in Autumn,
> Like a yellow water lily!
>
> . . . .
>
> Thus the Birch Canoe was builded
> In the valley, by the river,
> In the bosom of the forest;
> And the forest's life was in it,

All its mystery and its magic,
All the lightness of the birch-tree
All the toughness of the cedar,
All the larch's supple sinews;
And it floated on the river,
Like a yellow leaf in Autumn,
Like a yellow water-lily.

One of the contemporary writers on the wilderness whom I came to like very much was Calvin Rutstrum from Minnesota. He was a highly articulate, thoughtful old-timer who died only a few years ago. In his early writings, he mentions that his favourite canoe from long ago was a birchbark canoe built for him by Ojibway at Mille Lacs Lake in central Minnesota.

Rutstrum's philosophy of the wilderness is drawn in part from Thoreau and in part from his own canoeing experiences in the early part of the century in Minnesota and Ontario, during the course of which he often rubbed shoulders with the Ojibway.

His book *Once Upon the Wilderness*, a favourite of mine that I have read six or seven times, was begun in a cozy cabin that Rutstrum and his wife had built on Marchington Lake in northern Ontario. The railroad at the other edge of the lake was the umbilical cord that tied them to the "material-conscious, overpopulated, outside world." Early on in the book, Rutstrum announces his distaste for materialism and his value of leisure:

Something in the leisurely process of movement and periodical rests must have manifested itself strongly to me on these earlier trips and stayed with me, for I still crave a goodly share of leisure, and have consistently practiced it at whatever material or monetary sacrifice it incurred.

He says that the difference between urban and wilderness points of view is that from the latter tends to regard the news objectively and a little more philosophically. And the important thing for Rutstrum is that there seems to be more time to think in the woods:

> With a cabin stocked for the winter with sacks, caddies, and small tubs of staple foods, along with a deer, moose, or caribou hung in the meat cache, I felt rich and secure. Or, perhaps, I did not think about the hazard of insecurity at all, which had much to do with this staple food approach. Leisure time I have always regarded as a necessity too valuable to be easily negotiable.

But then Rutstrum trips up, I think. He says that Thoreau has had a growing influence on our way of life. True, Thoreau influenced Martin Luther King and Gandhi, and there was some Thoreauvian influence apparent in the 1960s. But one of his basic observations a century and a half ago was that the mass of men lead lives of quiet desperation. Has not that become worse?

According to Rutstrum,

> Thoreau offers the best examples of how the human caged animal – satisfied with the food and shelter he gets from his captors – fails to grasp the liberating values which Thoreau depicted.

Rutstrum concludes by saying that we can afford to slow down long enough to allow the more profound values of life to catch up with us.

◆

So I tried to practise a lifestyle in the woods in keeping with this philosophy – a lifestyle that, with its idiosyncrasies and problems, would appear to be fairly strange to some people.

I kept one window clean all the time to see what the weather was. I moved the cabin over four feet to take up the slack in the clothesline. When I took a bath, I didn't have to worry about dressing right away even though there were no curtains on the windows, as I had no neighbours anyway.

Once, as I was walking around like this just prior to putting my clothes on after a bath, the fire in the stove needed more wood. I lifted the lid to put a stick in, but just as I did so my penis touched the nearly red-hot iron top of the stove. I jumped two feet and on the way down gave serious thought to rejoining the Church.

I spent much time trying to learn the ways of the woods. Some of the lessons, however, were not happy ones. It is startling, for example, how much someone who has handled an ax for years can learn in a millisecond from mishandling an ax.

I tried to practise hospitality as a bush skill. I endeavoured to show my visitors that I considered their visit a favour, not a burden. Like Rutstrum, I was always pleased with how appreciative the Algonquin were of visitors:

> There is a delightful repose in the whole manner of the
> wilderness Indian. I soon came to respect their way of life
> and later to yearn deeply for their company.

Looking around the cabin, I assessed my material position. I did not have electricity. I did have an outhouse with a fine view of the lake. My water came directly in a bucket from the lake.

But I was far ahead of four billion people — at least — on the planet in terms of material possessions. I had a truck, all the food I wanted and needed, the money and time to travel freely to various countries, and money for clothes and books. In peace of mind I was immensely richer than hundreds of millions of people, particularly in North

America, who are so wired into the contemporary consumer society that both husband and wife have to work outside the home and have neither time nor money for significant travel, for instance.

Alone in the little cabin, my mind achieved an activity it would not have had elsewhere. I realize the potential for this to sound vain, but I was stunned at my mental powers. I think my mother would have been even more stunned. My experience confirmed an observation by Rutstrum:

It has been quite conclusively established that the cultural measure of a man is his self-sustaining ability to be alone a generous share of the time.

CHAPTER 14

Basil Smith came to my cabin on the lake occasionally and stayed a few weeks with me. We spent our time building birchbark canoes together. He rose early and worked late. After supper he might go out and work a little more on the canoe, but most often he would sit on the porch and delight in watching the beaver swim back and forth in quest of poplar. Sometimes, after a long while of sitting, he'd say, "*Gackawan*," and I would know without looking up from my book that the mist was starting to creep across the lake.

Basil was an unassuming man, and there was a lot to learn from him. That quality, among others, was well worth emulating.

His difficulty in hearing had started when he was with two of his brothers, Arthur and Paul, on a log drive in 1937. Basil was on the log jam planting the dynamite; his brothers were in the canoe.

Paul started to light the fuse. Someone forgot to close the box of caps and several sticks of dynamite under his seat blew up. Paul's body disappeared. Their father, Charlie Smith, set out to search for it and found Paul's body several days later in the river.

Basil Smith splitting spruce root on a mosquito-infested day.

Arthur recovered from the explosion. Basil suffered hearing loss and spinal injuries. The company paid for a pauper's funeral for Paul and gave the family two hundred dollars as compensation.

I thought, after a while with Basil, that I might have "caught" his partial deafness, not that there was anything contagious about it. I noticed that he often missed much ambient conversation. Perhaps I perceived some advantages to the condition.

At my cabin Basil and I had been making a canoe — "canoe" in this area was often synonymous with "birchbark canoe" — when we had visitors, six women and children from the reserve in Maniwaki. We put them up for the night. Basil quite readily, and of his own accord, took blankets and a pillow to the porch and slept contentedly on the hard floor, even though he was in his seventies. If I can achieve the same degree of serenity by the time I am in my seventies, I will have accomplished a lot. I liked his mobility, his versatility, and his taste for simplicity. Can the quietest people teach the most?

Sometimes I'd visit Basil when he was staying at a little log cabin on the shore of Bitobi Lake on the reserve near Maniwaki. The log construction was not of the punctilious sort that requires a mortgage on a significant part of one's life. This log cabin was the same size, sixteen feet by twenty feet, as mine. Though it was of logs and mine was a frame cabin, I realized the great attraction of our cabins was that they were sufficient.

Basil had been quite popular as a hunting and fishing guide, especially at Désert Lake, about forty miles northwest of Maniwaki. He had worked the longest there, where Jocko Carle was foreman of the guides.

Basil was guiding some tourists for fishing during the blueberry season. Amazed at the number of blueberries on shore, the twelve tourists in several canoes asked to debark to pick some. "Too bad we don't have a blueberry pie," one of the tourists lamented.

Basil set to work. They had some kind of big round container that was two inches deep. He asked another Indian to get a big sheet of birchbark. Then Basil borrowed a half-full whiskey bottle from one of the tourists and, using it, rolled out dough on the sheet of birchbark. The whiskey sloshed around in the bottle as he worked. He asked the same Indian friend to find a dead maple tree about two inches in diameter and to cut it up and make a hot fire.

When the fire had burned down, Basil buried the pie in the sand under the coals. Half an hour later, the tourists partook of fresh blueberry pie.

◆

William Commanda had some friends from the United States who regularly came up to western Quebec to go hunting and fishing. On one occasion, they had spent much effort and money hunting moose far in the woods, but to no avail. Desperate for a successful hunt, one of William's friends left their camp a hundred miles off in the woods and came all the way to William's house on the reserve to ask if William and Basil would come and guide for them. Everyone knows that Indians are perfectly at home and extremely capable in the woods. William and Basil packed their warm clothes, fetched their rifles, and rode back to the camp with their friend, who was confident that their chances of finding a moose had improved enormously.

Because it was late in the evening when they arrived, they had a good supper and went to sleep right away so that they could make an early start on the morrow. The next morning, it was barely starting to get light as the men finished breakfast and gathered their rifles. As they were about to leave the cabin, the unspoken thought of each of the Americans was that if anyone could help them to find a moose, it would be these two old Indian hunters.

When they opened the cabin door, two big moose were standing fifteen feet in front of them.

This anecdote is true, although it has all the elements of a shameless lie.

◆

For some reason, Basil seemed to have an unusual number of interesting experiences on his trapline, which was located in the southern part of La Vérendrye Wildlife Reserve. Basil did not have a motor vehicle, so he had to ask a friend to take him to his cabin. To travel back to the Maniwaki reserve, more often than not he would walk out to the highway and hitch a ride with a passing motorist.

One fall, he was picked up by an Indian friend who was going directly back to the Maniwaki reserve. As they motored down the highway, the man asked Basil a question relating to the fact that an Indian trapper had the right to shoot one moose on his trapping territory any time during the year.

"Say, Basil, have you shot a moose this year yet on your trapline?" the friend asked.

"No," Basil answered.

"Do you suppose it would be all right some time if I shot a moose on your trapping territory?"

"Why, sure," said Basil, with the effusive generosity for which he was well known.

The man started to put on the brakes and pulled onto the shoulder. "Good then. I just shot one twenty minutes ago. Let's turn around and go get it."

◆

One of his rides did not turn out so well. It was more than thirty below zero in December, and the snow had piled up in the bush so deep that Basil thought it was not worth trapping any longer. He snowshoed out to the highway and hitched a ride. He did not have long to wait. A man coming from the north picked him up.

Basil Smith trimming gunwale with an ax.

Thirty miles down the highway, they came to the first buildings, a restaurant and motel. A big surprise awaited them. In front of the motel, Quebec Provincial Police had made a massive roadblock: police cars were all across the road with their lights flashing, and the officers had their guns drawn. They were looking for a bank robber who had held up a bank in the north.

I am not sure Basil has ever completely become used to the things white society does, despite decades of rubbing shoulders with the other race. Basil was nervous because he had never seen such a commotion as a big roadblock for a bank robber. The driver of the car was nervous because he was the bank robber.

The police stopped the car, pulled Basil and the bank robber out, and ordered both of them to spread arms and legs and stand with their hands on the hood of the car. The metal was brutally cold.

Now, any trapper knows that you don't put bare hands on freezing metal when the temperature is thirty degrees below zero. So Basil reached into his coat pocket for his mittens. At this point an officer thought Basil was going for a pistol, so he quickly stuck a rifle barrel in Basil's ribs.

A waitress watching the drama from the restaurant suddenly recognized Basil and ran from the restaurant in her apron shouting, "Hey, that's Basil Smith; that's Basil Smith!" In minutes Basil was a free man again.

◆

Basil became better known – perhaps through a couple of my books – and from time to time a journalist would seek him out.

On one occasion, a journalist came from France and wanted to interview Basil, so Basil and I suggested that a favourite tavern in town would be a suitable place for an interview.

We had some brandy and beer as the journalist asked several

questions. Then he came to one very intriguing question. Now, I know what his question was and I know what Basil's answer was, but I can only guess at the thinking of each man. There was not one kind of logic there, but two. Each man considered the question quite reasonably.

The journalist asked Basil, "Mr. Smith, suppose you're walking on a lake in the winter in very cold weather and you accidentally fall through the ice. What do you do?"

The journalist may have been thinking that Basil might have a sheath knife and that he might pull it out quickly and use it as a pick to pull himself up on the ice and out of the hole.

Basil may have been thinking: this poor man asks me what I'm going to do if I fall through the ice in the winter. What does he expect me to do – try a little fishing in the hole? Smoke a cigar?

Basil's head turned quickly and he backed off a couple of inches, as if in surprise at the question. "Why, you get out, of course!" he exclaimed.

◆

Basil and I were hired a few years in succession to make birchbark canoes at the Canada Canoe Festival, held in Ottawa under the aegis of the National Capital Commission. Because of his warmth and gentleness, Basil was probably more popular than the canoe.

Making a birchbark canoe in those surroundings – a demonstration with thousands of people around – proved to be a decidedly new and interesting experience. The idea that the birchbark canoe seen in the early stages of construction would result in a fine finished canoe strained the credulity of many. One woman, who seemed well educated in everything but birchbark canoe construction, took a look at the bark sheet held up with stakes, the stones inside the assembly, the bark scraps and cedar chips strewn around and inquired, "Sir, is this an archeological dig?"

During my years in the bush, my main vocational activity was writing novels. Somehow though, I kept getting involved with birchbark canoes — writing about them, taking photos of them, or making them. But these activities often had an inadvertent character about them.

I also thought about women a lot, which is a case of impossible dreaming if ever there was one. The truth of the matter was plainly that the isolated situation in which I lived was not at all conducive to socializing with members of the opposite sex — unless, perhaps, I could occasionally induce a representative to come to visit. Nor did it seem especially wise to become involved with a woman who was foolish enough to want to get mixed up with me.

I recall a there-but-for-the-grace-of-God-go-I encounter that illustrates the difficulty of meeting a young woman from a town or city environment and attempting to integrate her into the bush life.

Bobby Tremblay was a young — in his thirties at the time — intelligent, good-looking fellow who lived on the edge of the bush in a log cabin without electricity or running water. Like me, he had tried to scale back in various ways. His cabin was not large and his material acquisitions were limited. He had a canoe and dogs and a sled, and led dogsled trips in the winter.

Coupled with a wish for a simple existence was his desire to meet a comely woman. As might be imagined, the average woman lived on a different material level than Bobby.

Claire Poirier, a distant cousin of his, worked at the outfitter's office in Maniwaki, just down from the bus stop. One day, a woman walked into her office asking if she knew whether a certain Bobby Tremblay was in town. Claire called around and it turned out that Bobby was in the village and would be sent over.

The woman was dressed to the nines — high heels, nice dress, the

Ernestine Gidmark, sitting on a log from which a single sheet of birchbark was taken.

works. She had met Bobby in Ottawa and was on her way up for a visit. Claire asked the woman if she knew where Bobby lived. The woman said she did not. Claire — perhaps wanting to preserve things for Bobby as long as possible — did not go into any explanation, but at the same time she wondered how long the relationship would last.

Bobby picked the woman up and took her to his cabin ten miles north. Not much more than an hour later, Claire saw Bobby dropping her off at the bus stop for the next bus to Ottawa.

When Bobby came into Claire's office, she asked him what had happened. It turned out that the woman had decided, rather quickly apparently, that Bobby's place wasn't to her taste. Among the observations she made was that there were no curtains on the windows of the log cabin. "I told her I didn't have any neighbours," said the hapless Bobby, "but that didn't seem to make any difference to her." And Bobby was left to try again a kind of hunting that is difficult under the best of circumstances.

As fortune would have it, I met a fine woman in 1985 in Ottawa, when Basil and I were making a birchbark canoe on Victoria Island in the Ottawa River.

We had finished making the canoe one afternoon of an arduous six-day building stint. The canoe was fourteen feet long and we had made it with a single sheet of birchbark, not needing to add any side pieces. We had just finished gumming it.

"Should we take it down to the water and paddle around a little to try it out?" I asked Basil.

"You take it; I want to rest," he answered.

I lifted the canoe onto my shoulders and walked the quarter-mile to the end of the island. And there I saw a most remarkable sight.

As if in some kind of romantic fantasy, there on the edge of the river sitting on a large rock was a very beautiful young Indian woman wearing a white dress.

I set the canoe down by the water's edge, perhaps ten feet from the young woman. When she wasn't looking, I looked at her.

She had a full mouth, lustrous black hair, strikingly alluring Indian eyes, and the high cheekbones of her race. She looked at me; I smiled. I picked up the paddle and took hold of the canoe by a gunwale to lift the canoe into the water. I hesitated, looked over at her and asked, "Would you like to go for a ride in the canoe?"

She smiled. I was to learn that that smile was characteristic of her. "Yes," she said.

There was only one paddle, so she sat just in front of the centre thwart while I paddled. We spoke little.

Back on shore, I asked her name — Ernestine. For a few moments I fidgeted around, trying to figure out how I could spend more time with her. Basil was expecting me to come back shortly.

"Will you be here for a while?" I asked.

"I'm going over to the totem-pole ceremony," she said.

I knew that a huge totem pole carved by some west coast Indians was going to be raised shortly. "Maybe I'll see you there," I said.

When I carried the canoe back to the canoe-building site, I told Basil about the totem-pole raising ceremony. Basil liked to socialize, but he took special occasions with a grain of salt. We walked over to where people were gathered for the event.

The forty-foot totem pole, made from an enormous cedar from British Columbia, had been carved as it lay on supports placed on the ground. A hole had been dug for the base of the totem pole and some high, solid uprights had been driven into the ground ready for the two big ropes that would be used to pull the pole upright. Fifty people grabbed each rope. Basil, Ernestine, and I were next to each other on one rope. Surprisingly, it seemed almost effortless to pull. "Look at that!" Basil said as we watched the top of the gigantic totem pole rise into the air.

I invited Ernestine for supper. During the meal, I learned that she was an Ojibway from Spanish River, about eighty miles east of Sault Ste. Marie, Ontario. As a child she spoke Ojibway, but was not able to speak the language when I met her because she had been taken from her family when she was very young.

After being raised by French-Canadian foster parents, Ernestine moved to Ottawa where she worked for several years. Among the things I learned about her later was that her grandfather, John Caibaiosai, had been a birchbark canoe builder. He built his canoes at the mouth of the Spanish River on Georgian Bay, part of Lake Huron.

Ernestine, though younger than I was, had been raised in a one-room cabin heated with a wood stove. There was no electricity or running water. Her mother, father, and five siblings lived in the same single room, roughly the size of my cabin — sixteen by twenty feet.

Basil Smith and Ernestine Gidmark with a canoe model he made.

When Ernestine's grandmother became old, they took her in as well.

Later that evening, Ernestine agreed to return with me to the cabin north of Maniwaki. She left a note for her sister saying that she was heading north, and the next morning got into the truck full of canoe-making gear along with Basil and me. She'd never been north of Ottawa before. She was impressed by the beauty of the Gatineau River flowing from the north with its log jams. It flowed through green hills. From time to time a small farm could be seen in the valley, along the river, or perched on one of the hills.

CHAPTER 15

Gradually I increased my contacts with the Algonquin in Rapid Lake, about sixty miles north of where I was living. Ernestine came with me when I went there, happy, I think, to be living again a kind of life she had not seen since Spanish River.

Rapid Lake was still sometimes known by the name of the community's former location, Lake Barrière. In the 1870s, it was established as a Hudson's Bay Company post, and the Algonquin in the area had assembled around the settlement, for the summer months at least.

The Indians at Lake Barrière had always been among the most nomadic of the Algonquin. They spent much of their time on their hunting grounds and a few of the summer months near the post. In 1877, Louis Christopherson was appointed apprentice postmaster there. It was he who later supervised the building of so many fur trade canoes, and it was from him that Adney obtained the most detailed technical information about them. Christopherson was later factor at Grand Lake Victoria, the Algonquin settlement fifty miles by canoe west of Lake Barrière.

David Makakons removing excess bark prior to beginning construction at Lake Barrière.

Lake Barrière had always been an isolated community. Into the 1920s, the Indians used to come down to Maniwaki, a hundred miles away, by birchbark canoe. One of the old men I knew could remember travelling in about the same year by birchbark canoe to North Bay, Ontario, to sell fur at auction there. It was a trip of nearly two hundred miles by canoe, one way.

In September 1928, the American anthropologist Frederick Johnson travelled to Lake Barrière. He had studied at the University of Pennsylvania under the famous anthropologist Frank Speck. At that time, the settlement was composed of about twenty-five families. When Johnson visited Lake Barrière, it took him twenty-two hours over two days to travel seventy miles. He went from Maniwaki to La Croix Springs (about a mile and a half north of our cabin) by truck, slept overnight, and then was taken by truck to a place called Half-Way. The road went around trees, down ungraded hills, through mud holes, over corduroy roads sometimes a mile long, and over shaking bridges. From Half-Way, Johnson walked for fifteen miles along the road to Bark Lake Depot, and travelled on to Lake Barrière by canoe.

The Lake Barrière band chief in 1928 was David Makakons, who remained chief until he died in 1964. He had worked all his life as a birchbark canoe maker. William Commanda knew him and told me that he was a fine orator. "He didn't speak a word of English or French," William said, "but you should have heard him speak in Indian."

In those days, because the band was so nomadic, David Makakons's authority generally was limited to the time the band was at the Hudson's Bay Company post at Lake Barrière.

These Indians traded for articles at the post, but, due to limited carrying capacity, few things could be taken with the families when they returned to their hunting grounds, and they soon had to depend again exclusively on moose meat.

At Lake Barrière, Johnson saw many birchbark canoes being used in 1928, but already there were a few canvas canoes with motors rigged to them.

In 1947, the government began to move this Indian community to Rapid Lake, about twenty-five miles from the old settlement and only a few miles off the main north-south highway.

My few visits to Rapid Lake revealed it to be a more Aboriginal settlement than nearly all the other reserves I had seen. The Department of Indian Affairs still has a hell-bent-for-leather plan to acculturate the Indians and so, I assume, is much more proud of some of these other reserves than of the one at Rapid lake. Government policy seems to be that the only good Indian is a white-educated Indian.

David Makakons, long-time chief at Lake Barrière, with one of his birchbark canoes. On the left is Charlie Smith, River Désert Algonquin, father of Mary Commanda and Basil Smith. When the photograph was taken, David was in his eighties and still making canoes. The wooden deck-pieces, an unusual feature, were typical of David's canoes.

The Rapid Lake community is history in the making, an illustration of how white culture is being shoved down the throats of the Indians. It exemplifies how white culture is being absorbed massively (and sometimes even voluntarily) through compulsory education in that culture, and through what might be called the great intravenous transfusion of white culture – television. Could there ever be a more effective medium for accomplishing acculturation?

The Department of Indian Affairs should be called the Department of White Man's Affairs because it is concerned much more with inflicting the white man's culture on the Indian than on preserving Indian skills and traditions.

Why is it that some people think that Indians are successful people only if they are successful in white men's terms? Why do we think the ideal Indian is one who has gone to grade school, high school, and college? Is only an Indian who graduates from college cause for rejoicing? When we have succeeded in luring him away from his ancient traditions, is it really success that has been achieved?

On one of my visits to Rapid Lake, I met four white teachers who taught in a small school there. They seemed to feel they were in exile.

The head teacher pointed out to me that although the teachers' houses and the Indians' houses had been built at the same time, the Indians' houses were dilapidated. He obviously wanted me to draw my own conclusions. I did. One of them was that we would probably have much more difficulty surviving in the woods than the Indians had making do with those houses.

One of the female teachers was teaching ballet to the Indian children. She was also an *aficionada* of cross-country skiing, a fad currently growing in popularity in eastern Canada. When asked whether she had tried snowshoeing – the people among whom she was living were among the finest makers and users of the snowshoe left on the continent – she replied, "But what fun do you see in that?"

There were still birchbark canoe makers at Rapid Lake, but the men with this skill were in the same position as Jocko Carle; they had worked as guides and trappers and had discontinued canoe making. As isolated as the Rapid Lake canoe makers were, their canoes were known. They were sometimes sold through the Poirier General Store in Maniwaki, and at other times buyers made the long trip to Rapid Lake.

The community at Rapid Lake, and at Lake Barrière before it, included many birchbark canoe makers. Perhaps because of the people's need for canoes, or because of the plentifulness of excellent material

Poirier General Store, Maniwaki, Quebec, 1940. The sign at left reads "Reliable Guides" and "Birch Bark Canoes For Sale." The canoes were by Patrick Maranda, David Makakons, Paul Matchewan and others from Lake Barrière.

for canoe construction in the area, the builders of Rapid Lake generally were regarded as more skilled than the Indian builders in nearby regions.

All the canoe builders admired Patrick Maranda. His canoes were characterized by an elegant sheer (top line) and a fairly straight rocker (bottom line), as well as by fine crooked knife work on the ribs and sheathing. Born in 1901, Patrick was one of the finest makers of the birchbark canoe in the last four decades. I met him a number of times, but I never saw him building. His canoe-making days were several years behind him by the time I came along. He walked slowly and had difficulty seeing. The loss of his wife a few years before had also contributed to the end of his canoe building; she had been his helpmate. When I visited Patrick, we spoke partly in Algonquin and partly in

English. As was the case with most of the older Indians from Maniwaki, the majority of the Indians at Rapid Lake could speak Algonquin, French, and English. It was fascinating to think what it might have been like to work with Patrick Maranda in his prime.

The most skilled Indian makers of birchbark canoes usually possess the complete range of unique attributes of their culture. The finest Indian builders I met, then and later spoke an Indian language as their first language and taught it to their children. They were exceptionally resourceful in the woods and needed to be there. And their fine work in birchbark canoe construction was inevitably accompanied by excellent workmanship in the making of snowshoes, cradle boards, and other items of Indian material culture. I wanted to identify the best living Indian makers of the birchbark canoe because they were men to be admired.

In August 1985, Ernestine and I went to Rapid Lake to meet John Ratt and Jim Jerome, two men who had started building birchbark canoes again. Alec Ratt, John's brother, also had built a birchbark canoe three years previously. For Ernestine, it was a chance to be in a strongly Indian environment again, something from which she had been disconnected for many years.

John Ratt and Jim Jerome were both willing to build birchbark canoes with us, but when we got there we found that John had been shanghaied into working on one of the band's housing construction jobs. His foreman was a white man. It was sad to think that one of the last good Indian makers of the birchbark canoe in North America was kept from making a canoe by the need to work as a carpenter for a few weeks. The skilled white foreman probably did not realize what was happening. Of course, he would have been hard put to do anything about it.

We left John on the construction job and walked the hundred yards to the house of Jim Jerome. Much to my surprise, one of his children

Jim Jerome's canoe building camp. The stick framework over the hole is for smoking hides.

told us that he was at that moment across the lake building a birchbark canoe. We waited until he returned to the settlement that evening and made arrangements to go with him and take photos the following day.

Jim had made his camp on a small point about a mile across the lake from the Rapid Lake settlement. The point was swept by the wind most of the day and this kept the mosquitoes away.

"We've been working on the canoe on and off for maybe two weeks," Jim said. "We don't work at it steady, you know, because we've got things to do across the way too." Jim's wife, Angèle, had been tending to household chores and sewing moccasins.

They had a tent on the narrow point just at the edge of the trees. The tent was a spacious canvas one, about ten by twelve feet. Jim had bought it used a few years before for fifteen dollars. He had fashioned a wooden floor of plywood and panelling. Jim and Angèle had a double bed on one side of the tent, and their son, Corey, had a bed opposite them. Out of an old gas tank from a big truck, Jim had welded a box stove. The stove pipe was wired up and went out the back of the tent. They had brought a small table from their house, and Jim had put up some makeshift shelving.

Elsewhere in the camp, not far from the canoe-building bed, was a fire pit for making an open fire and a dug-out fireplace for smoking hides. This little hole in the ground was covered by a domelike framework of alders over which the hide would be placed for smoking. Next to the large tent, there was a *tcicakwahiganatik*, the tree trunk of birch over which they placed the moose hide for smoking.

Corey was eleven years old and tall for his age. He had strong, expressive Indian features and invariably was smiling. When asked if he was going fishing, for example, he would smile first and then respond.

Fishing for walleyes was his passion. He'd sit out on the point for hours jigging for them. He would bring five or six fish back to the tent and Angèle would clean them. Because there was no refrigeration on the point, Angèle wrapped the cleaned fillets in newspaper and fixed them for the next meal.

Jim was a very patient man, and fairly hard of hearing, although he seemed to hear Angèle well when she was speaking quietly in Algonquin. I wondered whether his hearing problem might have resulted from many years of chainsaw use. Some of the chainsaws might not have had mufflers. I don't think Jim's outboard motor was the culprit. Although it was sixty years old – Jim never threw out something he could manage to keep working – it was quiet compared to some of the other engines in the area.

The canoe bed was located under some small birches that provided shade for the building area. Canoe makers often make such shelters. In Jim's time, shelters frequently were constructed of upright poles with a

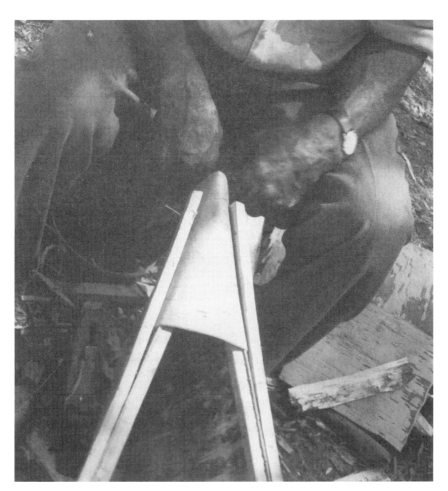

Jim Jerome fitting a bark deck-piece into the gunwale.

gabled roof. Bark sheets tawny sides down covered it, and small sticks were placed on top to keep the bark down. The roof could be birchbark, spruce bark, or cedar bark. "Cedar bark is the best there is," Jim said.

At the time of my visit Jim was sixty-seven, and he walked slowly with a slight limp in his right leg. His hair was close-cropped on the sides and combed back on top. He was very solicitous of our welfare, making sure that Ernestine and I had a foam mattress to put in the tent and also that I had a second, and sometimes third, helping of Angèle's cooking.

Ernestine seemed to be in her element. Having been taken from her family and raised by white people, and having spent so much time in the city, she was happy to be in the woods again with these fine Indian people.

Jim had gone to Barrière Dam, not far from the old Lake Barrière settlement, to get bark for this canoe. He lamented, as do all of the living builders of the birchbark canoe, that suitable bark was becoming scarce. I thought that it was the Indian canoe makers who truly were becoming scarce.

He said that good bark was white with thin green moss on it. Bark that peeled in August had to be good, he said, otherwise it would not peel very easily. Even before the advent of the chainsaw, the birch tree was cut down to take the bark off the tree for a canoe. In those days, they did their cutting with an ax and either a crosscut saw or a bucksaw.

When Ernestine and I arrived at the point, the temporary sheathing was already in place in the bottom of the canoe, and Jim was in the process of bending the ribs. His fire was about ten feet from the canoe. For soaking the ribs, he used an old drainpipe closed at the bottom with a tin can. He stuck the closed end in a fire of four-foot birch logs and wired the other end up to a post he had stuck into the ground.

Having placed all the ribs across the gunwales, he marked the ribs three finger lengths in from the gunwale. He bent them two at a time, starting from the centre thwart and working first toward one end of the canoe and then toward the other.

Jim then put the binder in place and continued to adjust the ribs so that they were perfectly vertical and fitted snugly against the bottom of the canoe. To do this, he tapped each rib sideways a little along the bottom, or used his hammer to tap down the end of the rib.

There are many parts to a birchbark canoe, and ideally all should be well finished. Anyone who has seen many birchbark canoes soon learns to discern whether the wood has been well carved with the crooked

The gunwale of Jim Jerome's canoe.

knife, whether the spruce root has been split and lashed evenly, and whether the sheer and rocker lines are fair. Perhaps the most telling thing about the quality of birchbark canoe construction is something I noticed immediately about Jim Jerome's canoe: when the ribs were bent and held in the canoe by the binder, they were nearly perfect with no uneven bends, and they fitted snugly in the bottom of the canoe with only the binder holding them down. It was obvious that Ernestine and I were in the presence of a very good canoe maker.

Jim left the canoe about seven in the evening the first day we were on the point. He and Angèle spent the night at the campsite, but first they went home to fetch some supplies. We rode back with them and went to see John Ratt.

John was working on the motor of his car when we arrived. His wife, Emilie, was sitting in the passenger's seat, apparently waiting for

John's results. We stayed with John and Emilie that night. Over a glass of brandy, a libation much favoured by canoe makers, John and I had a chance to talk.

He told me he had made eight birchbark canoes in his life, including four in the last ten years. It surprised me that he had made so few, as the one I had seen was of good workmanship. He had also made many canvas canoes.

John was sixty-three years old and Emilie was fifty-two. I asked how many children they had. John looked rather perplexed and turned to Emilie, and after a suitable deliberation, she came up with the number eleven.

John's father, Abraham, was chief of the band at one time and also a canoe maker. It was from him that John learned how to make a birchbark canoe. I had heard about a number of canoe makers who were caught in the bush after spring trapping without a canoe to use for the return trip. John was one of them. When it happened to him, he made a canoe in four or five days, using nails on the gunwale. Such exploits seem to be rather common among the Rapid Lake canoe makers.

John lamented the fact that the young people in Rapid Lake were not interested in birchbark canoe making. "The young don't want to learn because they go to school," he said. For him, the two facts had a direct connection. In the old days, he said, most men could make canoes. It was part of the usual complement of bush skills.

While in Rapid Lake, I tried to practise my Algonquin, though the Rapid Lake version of the language was significantly different from the Maniwaki Algonquin, and caused me some difficulty. There was an accent and an intonation that, I think, rendered Rapid Lake Algonquin rather difficult even for the River Désert Algonquin in Maniwaki. No matter where the speaker came from, I fought a continual battle with the grammar.

An Indian woman in Rapid Lake was skinning a moose. I couldn't get the grammatical form for "Where did you kill the moose?" so the best I could do was to come up with a lame, "How did the moose die?"

And when I met a little five-year-old from Rapid Lake, it was only too clear that he spoke Algonquin with a command that I could perhaps never attain. I was in awe of his ability to handle the grammar.

The next day before sunrise, Jim started work on the gunwale caps. When he finished, he put them in the water to soak.

Jim, who learned birchbark canoe making from his father, John, had made about twenty birchbark canoes in his lifetime. His uncle, Noël Jerome, and many other relatives in Rapid Lake, were also birchbark canoe makers. Jim's father and uncle and their families used to live at a little isthmus on Lake Andostagan. There, around the turn of the century, they built fur trade birchbark canoes. When they'd finished one, they'd paddle it to the post at Lake Barrière — a two days' trip — where they'd sell it to the Hudson's Bay Company factor.

According to Jim, only a few decades ago roughly three-quarters of the men at Rapid Lake were capable of making a birchbark canoe, which seems a very high number when compared to other reserves. At that time, however, canoes were the only transportation the Rapid Lake Indians had, and so knowing how to make one was an essential skill.

It was in the 1940s that Jim last used birchbark canoes to any great extent. When he was a young boy, he sometimes put a tarpaulin up in a birchbark canoe to use as a sail. "It was a lot easier than paddling," he said. He remembered going as a child of ten in 1928 with his parents and others in two birchbark canoes to Maniwaki, more than a hundred miles south by water, to get supplies. Up until the 1960s, for winter transportation Jim had used one or two dogs pulling a sled.

One March in the mid-1960s, Jim had gone out to his cabin near Brûlé Lake, a couple of days' journey by canoe from Rapid Lake. He had travelled there over the snow with two dogs pulling his sled. When the ice went out, that mode of travel was no longer suitable. He therefore built a fourteen-foot birchbark canoe out of a single piece of bark. He used no spruce root to lash the gunwales, only nails. It took three days. He carried his dogs and duffel away from Brûlé Lake at the end of May to the cabin of another Indian who had a truck. They drove to Rapid Lake. "They carry a lot, birchbark canoes, you know. Damn right they do."

Queried as to why the young people were not learning birchbark canoe making from the older men, Jim said, "Young people are too interested in all these foolish things that are coming out every day. They don't pay any attention to the old routine."

Jim put the canoe in the sun early in the morning, so that the ribs would dry during the day. Then he began to make the sheathing, for which he cut the cedar on a point of land one-half mile from the village.

It was interesting to see that, even though Algonquin canoes closely resembled each other in most respects, the builders with whom I worked sometimes had different ways of achieving the same result. Jim did the initial splitting of the cedar blank with a birch mallet and two birch wedges, and sometimes he used an ax. When the blanks were perhaps one inch thick, he did the fine splitting with a strong-bladed knife. As soon as the split was begun, he continued it by hand. When the split looked like it was about to run too much in one direction, he applied pressure in the opposite direction to bring the split back to the centre. He worked along with his hands all the way to the end of the blank. If he needed a little leverage to work the blank, he used a fork in a tree. When Jim finished splitting the sheathing, he planed the pieces, some with the crooked knife and some with a hand plane.

His next step was to remove the ribs from their temporary placement in the canoe. First he made a pencil mark on the outside of the ribs at the top of the gunwale, then he put them aside in two bunches, one for each half of the canoe. Next he removed the binder from the canoe.

At one end of the canoe, Jim used his crooked knife to trim the

Cutting the bark to the bow profile.

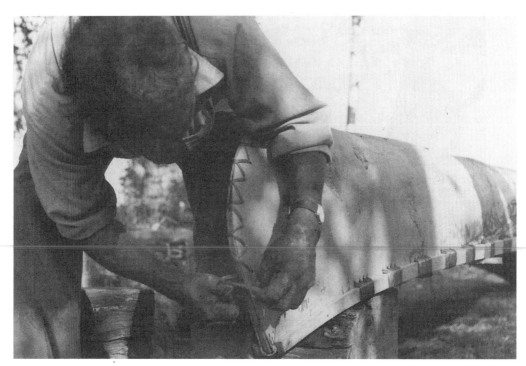

Jim Jerome lashing the bow of a birchbark canoe.

bark back to the stem-piece so that the two bark sheets would not come together when the end was sewn. The stem-piece would remain visible. For the other end, he turned the canoe upside down, evidently finding it easier to work this way.

Beginning with a length of spruce root about eight feet long, Jim did the lacing with a cross-stitch. While he was finishing the lacing on the second end of the canoe, Angèle started a fire and put a tin of tar on to melt. Her participation in the actual canoe making included preparing some spruce root and sewing it along the gunwales, and applying tar, which Jim sometimes used instead of spruce gum.

Angèle did all the cooking and washing for Jim while they were on the point. She was forty-four years old and was Jim's second wife, his first having died some years before. Her two great fears were frogs and bears. To avoid problems with bears, she took a chamber pot into the tent. The frogs were another matter. For some reason, she was quite afraid of them and would let out a shriek whenever she was walking around the camp area and came upon one. I asked her whether she feared bears more than frogs, and she could not make up her mind.

When she was free of housekeeping chores, she sat in the breeze on the grassy point and sewed moccasins. She had tanned moose hide some time before and used this to make moccasins, which she sold for the reasonable price of ten dollars. Some of the home-tanned hide had been coloured with smoke; the rest, although home tanned, had been coloured with a commercial dye that was a bit pinkish and did not look quite as attractive. The moccasins were lined and had beadwork on the tongue.

Corey did not speak when I first spoke to him. "*Ki cakwenim,*" I said. "You are shy." His blush showed that he was. Once his reticence was overcome, Corey could hardly stop talking and was eager to visit.

His great diversion on the point was a four-wheeled, all-terrain vehicle. Jim used it to draw four-foot birch logs from the bush to feed the fire he so often needed. For Corey, it was a little bit of Disneyland in the bush.

One of Corey's other pastimes was chasing a chicken they had brought over from the settlement. They did not leave it at their house while they were making the canoe because the chicken often escaped, and the dogs in the settlement would not be likely to show it any mercy. So the chicken was part of the canoe-making entourage, and from time to time the soughing of the breeze in the trees would be broken with calls from Corey running after the chicken — "*Pakakwan! Pakakwan!* Chicken! Chicken!"

There was some fear that a visiting skunk would set out after the chicken, but the fowl wisely roosted high in a tree and seemed to be away from harm. Its first night on the point was a dangerous one. The wind hit the unprotected point at more than fifty miles an hour. Our tent fell down twice. I could only imagine spending the night in a tree. When we went back to the settlement the next night, the chicken was enclosed in a brown paper grocery bag so that it would not jump out of the boat.

◆

Angèle applied tar to the inside of the canoe with a wooden spatula. She tarred the gores and then placed a two-inch strip of canvas over the tar. The birchbark canoe was to be well sealed from the inside as well as from the outside. Jim said that tar was easier to work with than spruce gum because it stayed soft longer. He had often used gum from the white spruce and the black spruce.

Jim began fitting the sheathing pieces up along the stem-piece in the bow of the canoe. Angèle made a fire and began to make bannock, as she had forgotten to bring bread from the village the night before. When the fire was going well, Jim hung a five-gallon pail of water over it. He would use the water later, applying it to the bark cover when inserting the ribs. Again he propped up the drainpipe that was used in bending the ribs. He took the gunwale caps out of the lake and put them both in the pipe. Because they were about fourteen feet long, they extended well out of the six-foot pipe and had to be supported against a branch.

The first rib Jim inserted in the canoe was the one inboard of the end thwart. He skipped the rib outboard of the thwart, which he would put in later. With his crooked knife, he bevelled the ends of the first rib and inserted it, forcing it in with the hammer. He did not drive it all the way in but left it slightly off the vertical, waiting until later, when he would also be using the hot water to help the bark adjust, to drive it home.

When all the ribs were partially driven home, he took the big bucket from the fire and poured the hot water into the canoe. He tipped the

Pounding ribs to the vertical in the bow.

canoe from side to side, sloshing the hot water around so that it would wet the sheathing and bark beneath it. He let the canoe sit for half an hour before he began hitting home the ribs to the vertical.

The gunwale caps were still in the steaming tube, although the fire had long since gone out. Angèle was sewing moccasins, so I was enlisted to help place the caps.

Jim measured one cap at a time, making sure it was long enough for the canoe. When he found the midpoint of the gunwale cap, he marked it and centred it in the middle of the lashing at the end of the centre thwart. I held the cap on Jim's left while he pounded a nail through it and into the gunwale below.

In the tradition of the Rapid Lake canoe, the gunwale cap first curved inboard to the end thwart and then outboard from the end thwart to the tip of the bow. It was nailed every eight inches or so.

Jim Jerome's finished canoe showing the tarred seams.

Once in a while, the nail was driven into the spruce root lashing, which did not seem to cause Jim any regret, although generally he tried to avoid doing so. The caps came to a point at the tip of the bow and at the end of the deck piece.

When the caps were in place, we took a break for supper: a large pan of moose meat, bannock, butter, and potatoes. A side dish was moose nose. This was scalded in the fire, then the charred surface was scraped off. It was scalded and scraped again until ready. Since I had tried moose nose before, I was quite content to settle for the main dish.

For the sealing of the outside seams of the canoe, Jim used a tar that was more viscous than the tar he used inside. He explained that he wanted a soft tar on the outside. He usually made his canoes with

Corey Jerome's chicken.

spruce gum. In fact, he said, he had a lot of white pine trees tapped for gum. He and Angèle, however, did not have time to collect the pine gum so he was using tar. He applied the tar with a wooden spatula he had fashioned from a piece of cedar. He smoothed it down with a moistened thumb.

In between short periods of giving Jim a hand with the canoe, I took many photographs. Never in the history of the Rapid Lake settlement had the residents seen anyone take five pictures of each part of a birchbark canoe.

Corey was almost as diligent in chasing the chicken as I was in taking photos. I would no sooner get set up for a photo than the chicken would come along, running for its life, with Corey hot after it.

One can study something to death. In fact, the subject doesn't even have to be near death before one has gone too far. People who later

Jim Jerome's finished canoe.

make use of one's material appreciate meticulousness, of course. But the compiler, in his attempt to record every last detail, may neglect to smell the roses.

"*Wekonen wendji ki kakige mäsinâtaman wîkwâs tcîmân?*" Corey asked, perplexed. "Why are you always taking pictures of the birchbark canoe?"

"Well, I don't know. It's something interesting, I guess."

"Why don't you take pictures of something else once in a while?" he asked.

"Like what for example?"

"Like my chicken."

"Your chicken?"

"Isn't my chicken just as important as the canoe?"

The construction of the birchbark canoe has many ramifications that bear on technology, history, and ethnology. For me, this was the first time that a philosophical question had been introduced into the matter of birchbark canoes. I was forced to think about it a moment. And the more I thought about it, the more trouble I had figuring out

Alec Ratt and his wife at Lake Barrière in 1985.

why a birchbark canoe was more important than a chicken. So I took a picture of the chicken.

Work on the canoe ended about nine in the evening that day. Jim was satisfied with the canoe and happy that the bark had been so good. The one thing he regretted was that the bark had not been wide enough and so had necessitated much extra work sewing the side panels.

For Ernestine, it had been a chance to immerse herself in Indian culture, an experience that had been missing from her life since the time, now distant in her memory, when she was with her mother and father in the woods as a very young child.

When we were at Rapid Lake visiting John Ratt and working with Jim Jerome, I heard an intriguing thing. John told me that his brother Alec was still using a birchbark canoe up at the old settlement at Lake Barrière.

We drove the forty miles up the bush road to the old Barrière

Alec Ratt's canoe (shown with his neighbour) at the former Hudson's Bay Company post at Lake Barrière, September 1985. When the photograph was taken, this 14-foot canoe was one of the few birchbark canoes in North America still being used by Indians for hunting and trapping.

settlement. There, a cluster of log cabins was inhabited by a few families. Alec was not there, but his neighbour took me to the canoe. We moved it out from the edge of the bush where it was stored and I took photos of it.

The fourteen-foot canoe itself was not particularly impressive, although it was quite well made. What struck me was that this birch-bark canoe was still being used by the Algonquin for hunting and trapping, the uses for which it had been devised by the Indians perhaps millennia ago. It was a tangible manifestation of the long life of the Indian canoe.

In other types of canoes, much is lost in aesthetics, and not just in the matter of materials. Though cedar strip canoes and wood and canvas canoes are attractive in comparison with aluminum and fibreglass ones, they don't match those made of birchbark and cedar, the feel of which is extraordinary. But it is especially in the lines that other canoes are lacking when compared with Indian canoes. Who would say otherwise when canvas or aluminum canoes are juxtaposed with the Algonquin old-style and *wâbanäki tcîmân* canoes, a well-made Ojibway long-nose, or the Malecite and the Abnaki canoes?

In writing about birchbark canoes, I include the builders' names. Doing so is not of great ethnological value, and it won't raise these people from the dead, but I thought I ought to.

Occasionally, if I became a little blasé, something would come along that would excite the spirit once again. One such spark was the following story, which was collected by a visitor to Grand Lake Victoria in 1926 and published in the *Journal of American Folklore*. Reading it finally gave me, after fifteen years spent with the Algonquin birchbark canoe builders, an idea of why it was so difficult to find good birch bark. The story speaks of a being named Meso.

> When the Indians first learned to use birch bark for canoes and utensils, Meso foresaw the possibility of the Indians utilizing all the trees in the forest. He was afraid that if good building bark could be found on every birch tree, the Indians would become extravagant and would not take care of the things they made. He feared that the Indians would throw things away while they were still useful and that they would make no effort to find those which had become lost. It appeared to him that the Indians would never become thrifty as long as there was a good supply of bark on every tree. All the trees would soon be cut down and that would mean the end of the forest upon which the Indians and the game were dependent for so much. Meso, therefore, climbed into many of the birch trees and swayed them about until their trunks became crooked and twisted. This he did to protect the forest. He also took a balsam bough and switched many of the trees. He scarred many of them so much that it is now difficult to find one which

will yield a suitable piece of bark large enough to make even a birchbark box.

Ernestine and I continued to see Jim and Angèle from time to time after that first long visit. Often Jim would stop on his way to Maniwaki for supplies. I have a clear memory of a time the following year when he came to stay a few days at our cabin so that we could look for bark together.

Because it was desirable to have a hot day and sunshine to harvest bark, I had listened intently to the radio report the night before.

I slept quite soundly despite my excitement at going with Jim the next day. Somehow, through the dreams and sleep, I heard Jim start to make the fire and then put on the radio. I was vaguely aware that it was time to make some effort to move.

Now, our bed is soft and unusually comfortable and getting out of it has, at times, taken a Herculean effort. I cocked one eye open and saw to my great discouragement that there was no sun. Great expectations of a sunny day in which to harvest bark were dashed. Then I directed my one open eye to the clock and realized that I was once again in the company of an Indian birchbark canoe builder of the ilk of Jocko Carle: there was no sun because it was 4:45 a.m.

CHAPTER 16

Ernestine had forgotten much of her Indian language. At the cabin, we worked hard studying it. We adopted a routine of speaking to each other only in Indian from the time we rose in the morning until six in the evening. Each infraction of this discipline, that is, using an English word, was punishable by the payment of a fine of twenty-five cents, which was given to a third party.

We added three new words a day to a vocabulary list numbered with the days of the month. It was important to list only common words that we did not know, for trying to learn uncommon words meant that they would never be used.

We played Scrabble in Indian; we read a paragraph from the Bible out loud, and then took turns giving each other a dictation with the same paragraph. We tested each other on sections of the Cuoq grammar, and placed a strong emphasis on the systematic, though highly complex, Algonquin verb. As an aural exercise, we listened to a religious tape made by a group in California. William Commanda had given it to me in hopes that some of its teachings would rub off on me. I hope some of it did, too — the language. William was one of the speakers on the tape. The others, most of them quite clear, were Algonquin from Maniwaki, Rapid Lake, and Lake Simon. I had never encountered anything recorded in Algonquin before, so it was a valuable resource. I think it helped a good deal, but it is a little odd to work with a tape like this and then meet a native speaker and try to start a conversation with a phrase such as "Christ rose from the grave."

Each of us kept a journal in Algonquin of the things we did daily. Thus we were well set up to go at the language from several different directions.

If all of this sounds wonderfully exemplary in terms of discipline, it is because it truly does sound wonderfully exemplary in terms of discipline. It didn't work out quite that well in actual practice because I had this terrible proclivity for procrastination. I wrote in the mornings and studied Algonquin in the evenings. The study of the Indian language was actually more important intellectually to me than writing, but writing was easier than studying Indian. Anything was easier than studying Indian.

So I would put it off far too often. To avoid the really difficult discipline, studying Algonquin, I would do almost anything else — split firewood, clean the cabin, even take a bath.

Ernestine's real apprenticeship in Indian culture started with Irene Jerome of Rapid Lake.

Irene was in her early fifties and lived about forty miles north of Rapid Lake at a place the Rapid Lake Indians called Kokomisville (Grandmother City). She lived there with her mother, Lina Nottaway, and various relatives at a little clearing in the woods by a lake. There were seven or eight log cabins there, some fairly large.

Irene stopped by our place one day on her way back from Maniwaki to pick up Ernestine. With her in the van were her son, Eddie, and

Sharon, an anthropologist from a state university in New York who was studying education of Indian children in Rapid Lake.

Ernestine packed her clothes while I served tea to the visitors. Irene was an assertive, intelligent woman with the kind of sense of humour that was ripe for teasing, so I teased her at every opportunity.

I told her that life was much better with a partner, and I would take it upon myself to find a man for her.

"I don't need a man!!" she shouted back, having been that route a time or two.

I told her that her protestations would not deter me from trying to help her out in that regard.

"Don't you dare!" she shouted as I kissed Ernestine goodbye.

Eddie drove up to Rapid Lake. In their van, they had the month's food supply — ten pounds of flour, some cases of milk and some of eggs, a five-gallon pail of lard, a five-pound roll of bologna, and a ten-pound slab of bacon. People from Rapid Lake usually made a monthly trip for supplies to Maniwaki, unless something like a doctor's appointment brought them down more often.

From Rapid Lake, they went north on the highway about thirteen miles and then turned off east on the bush road that lead to Nanouatan, which is the real name of Kokomisville. Irene's cabin was the biggest in the settlement. Made in the *pièce-en-pièce* fashion that the Rapid Lake Indians favoured, the cabin was twenty by forty feet. The rafters and the ridge pole were the only logs in the building longer than ten feet. The kitchen was walled off from the rest of the house and occupied about a third of the building. The rest was a large room that had two sofas and four beds. The kitchen was heated by a big woodstove and the main room by a box stove when it was cold. The refrigerator ran on propane, and light came from white-gas lanterns.

When they arrived, Irene went into the cabin and lit two lanterns so that they would be able to see as they unloaded the van. Eddie,

Sharon, and Ernestine each chose a bed and went to sleep after the unpacking was done.

Irene rose first the next morning, and Ernestine and Sharon got up when they smelled the coffee brewing. It had been raining all night, and it was still raining. Irene had to leave for a doctor's appointment in Val d'Or, but before she could go, she had to skin a moose that her son-in-law had shot a few hours before. He had drawn it from the woods and left it for Irene to skin.

While Irene and Sharon started to skin the moose, Ernestine watched over their shoulders to see how it was done. In the time Sharon had been at Kokomisville, she had helped to skin five moose, but she still had a difficult time.

Sharon skinned one hindquarter of the moose and Ernestine skinned the other. After the hide was completely off the moose, Irene went to find a sharp ax and four sharp knives with which to butcher the animal.

She first quartered it, and then Irene and Ernestine each took a quarter to a nearby table. Irene showed Ernestine how to take the meat off the bones by following the membrane of the moose. "Don't be afraid to cut the meat," she told Ernestine. They cut choice roasts and other parts.

They took sponge baths after their work and headed north to Val d'Or for Irene's doctor's appointment.

Their errands done, they made the long trip back to Kokomisville with a fine moose meat supper on their minds. It was not to be, though; Irene's son-in-law who had shot the moose had come back in the interim and taken all the meat. He hadn't even left them a roast. Ernestine fixed wild rice and bologna for supper.

Later that evening, the women worked on moccasins and a *tikinâgan*, or baby carrier. Irene's son-in-law had made the *tikinâgan*, and Sharon the anthropologist was fixing the calico cloth to the frame. She had already been at it a couple of weeks. As she knitted socks for her children and grandchildren for Christmas, Irene told Ernestine how in earlier years she used to make socks using the sleeves of old sweaters. By sewing the feet onto the sweater sleeves, she didn't have to spend money on more wool.

Irene talked about when she was younger and used to use "the old man's" crooked knife. Whenever she talked about "the old man," Ernestine knew she was talking about Patrick Maranda. As a young girl, Irene spent most of her time at his house. She learned how to make toy bows and arrows and, as she got older, ax handles and stretchers for stretching beaver hides. Patrick's wife would get mad at Irene and tell her not to use his knife, but he would tell her to keep on using it so she would learn how.

◆

The next morning, Irene outfitted Ernestine with rubber boots, plastic pants to go over her blue jeans, and an old shirt. This was the outfit Ernestine was to wear to take the hair off the moose hide prior to tanning it. She was a little trepidatious, but Irene had told her that she would become used to the smell of the moose when they were skinning it. Irene also warned Ernestine that she would probably find the work back breaking and that she'd certainly have a sore back in the morning.

They removed the heavy moose hide from the barrel of water where it had been soaking and carried it over to a peeled birch scraping log. Set at an angle of thirty degrees, the log was held up on one end by two legs that could be adjusted for height to suit the person doing the scraping.

Irene and Ernestine laid the hide with the hair side up on the scraping log, with the front legs of the hide closest to Ernestine. The knife for scraping had a dull edge so she would not cut the hide.

Irene demonstrated how to scrape the hair off the hide, an activity that requires a great deal of strength. When Ernestine had the hair side of the hide completely scraped, Irene would show her how to scrape the meat and sinew from the meat side of it.

Anthropologist Sharon was working on another hide, which she had draped over a pole and was wringing out.

It took Ernestine about two hours to remove the hair from the hide. She told me that the hair came off quite easily, which surprised me because I had always had difficulty scraping a hide. You can soak a hide in lime to make the hair come off more easily, but this generally is not done during tanning as the lime can damage the hide slightly.

While Ernestine and Sharon worked on the hides, Irene's mother, Lina, was driving around on her four-wheel, all-terrain vehicle with her small dog sitting behind her. She was checking snares she had set for rabbits and was on the look-out for good birchbark for baskets.

Lina was much like her daughter Irene – a bit fiery and opinionated. She told Ernestine that the snares were set but that she wasn't really hunting (the Rapid Lake people always used the word "hunting" for what we would call trapping), she was just puttering around. She said if she wanted to catch rabbits with snares, she would do it to mean business and she would get rabbits, but she was setting her rabbit snares to keep herself busy.

The Rapid Lake people, in keeping with other Woodland Indians, engaged in almost continuous hunting at certain times of the year, just as we go frequently to the supermarket. They needed the meat; it was that simple. One intriguing difference is that their meat has less cholesterol. Moose, muskrats, rabbits, and beaver engage in more exercise than domestic animals.

From time to time, Irene came over to check out the hide and see how Ernestine had done. They turned the hide over so the meat side was up, and Irene demonstrated how to remove any meat or muscle.

Ernestine continued to work, stretching from time to time because her back was becoming sore. Two hours later, Irene called from the

Pièce-en-pièce style construction favoured by the Rapid Lake Indians. They construct a large house in only a few weeks.

cabin that lunch was ready. Ernestine washed her hands but left her rubber boots and plastic pants on. She sat downwind during lunch because she smelled terrible.

During lunch, Sharon complained about the tough time she was having with her hide. In the second week of June, Irene had scraped a small hide and given it to Sharon to finish. She had put it in the water and had taken it out more than once. It was now the end of September.

I arrived for a visit the next day. As I helped Ernestine scrape the moose hide, she filled me in on some of Sharon the anthropologist's adventures. We are all prone to making generalities on the basis of anecdotes, and these generalities can be very unreliable. When Ernestine told me this story about Sharon, I fought against making any rash judgements about anthropologists.

Sharon's project was to look into the Indian methods of education, and it seemed that she herself was continually becoming educated in the most interesting ways.

The previous winter, she had been out trapping with Irene and her two sons. They were crossing a lake on their snowmobiles, Sharon's snowmobile at the end of the line. One of Irene's sons pulled his snowmobile out of line to talk to Sharon. "When we get to the edge of the lake, you'll have to accelerate a little to get up the bank at the shoreline," he told her.

Sharon accelerated a little too much. The snowmobile easily made the bank but the trajectory and speed Sharon had established sent the snowmobile up in the air high into the branches of a white spruce. Irene's two sons took it down from the tree.

One of the most useful activities one can do is to dream. Though I continued to listen, my mind was wandering considerably as Ernestine was talking about Sharon's adventures.

It is said that, in Canada, the average Indian family is composed of three members – the mother, the father, and the anthropologist. In the vagaries of my thinking, I came to the realization that I had read a considerable amount written about Indians by anthropologists. But I had never read anything anyone had written about anthropologists themselves. From the way Ernestine was describing Sharon, it became clear that anthropologists might be a much more interesting group than I had heretofore imagined. So I took some notes.

At the time of our visit, Irene was only just over fifty, but it was enjoyable to talk to her over tea about the old days. Years before she had gone with her family by birchbark canoe to Senneterre, Clova, and Grand Lake Victoria, places fifty to a hundred miles distant from Barrière. She saw birchbark canoes and canvas canoes at Grand Lake Victoria when she was there in the 1940s.

Her mother, Lina, told me that she used moose fat in the spruce

Patrick Maranda and his first wife, Monique, with a model canoe he made, c. 1950.

gum as a tempering agent when she was helping with a birchbark canoe. She said she liked orange or white gum, not black. She liked to get the gum when it came from a white spruce where the bear scratches the tree to get gum to make its bowels move in the spring. The spruce gum has the same effect on humans. Lina waited for two years after the bear does the scratching to gather gum from the wound in the tree. She said that in later years, the Indians used roofing tar to gum the canoes.

We spoke about Patrick Maranda. He was called *Nimicom* (Grandpa) and was remembered as a good, patient teacher. Patrick was the one many of the Indians went to for help when they didn't know a word in their own language. He gave birchbark canoe building classes in

Pierre Elliott Trudeau, prime minister of Canada from 1968 to 1979 and from 1980 to 1984, in 1974 in a birchbark canoe made by Patrick Maranda.

Rapid Lake in the 1970s. Other items he made were wooden puzzles, sleighs, toboggans (of maple or yellow birch), spoons, shovels, and *tikinâgans*.

Down the hill behind his house at Rapid Lake Patrick made canoes. On an island, he also had a cabin where he used to make birchbark canoes. It would take him about two weeks to make one. He would cut a tree down to get the bark, even if he had to do so with an ax.

On one of the occasions when I visited Patrick a few years before he died, I showed him a photo of Pierre Trudeau in one of Patrick's canoes. Although his eyesight was failing badly, by holding the photo very close he could see that the canoe was one of his. I then asked him if he recognized the man in the canoe. He said that he did not. When I asked him if he had ever heard of Pierre Trudeau, Patrick responded politely that he had not.

I helped Irene make some floaters of cedar for her fishnet. They were like bowling pins about fourteen inches long with a notch on the small end where it was affixed to the net. Weights for the fishnet were made by tying rocks in one-foot-by-one-foot squares of plastic garbage bags.

Irene had a little metal box with sand in the bottom that she used to smoke fish. She made the fire with rotten maple or maple bark for flavour.

Eddie arrived in camp from duck hunting. Irene cleaned the four ducks he brought and saved the feathers, which she would use later on for feather quilts for her beds.

When Ernestine finished her moose hide, Irene taught her how to make moccasins and on them, the floral designs of the Woodland Indians.

I spoke to Irene as often as I could about the days not long before when the Rapid Lake people had a very tough existence.

Once when a woman was about to give birth, her cervix began dilating early. It was in the winter so she was taken eighteen miles out to the highway on a toboggan pulled by dogs. There she and her companions waited for a ride on a passing truck that would take her to the hospital in Maniwaki or Val d'Or.

But what I enjoyed most of all was when Irene talked about the old canoe makers – Patrick Maranda, Paul Matchewan, and the old chief, David Makakons, who died in 1964.

During one winter, seven of David Makakons's children died of tuberculosis. After contact with European civilization, the rate of infant mortality in Native communities was horrendous. The Barrière Indians claimed that children never died of exposure, but rather of

The author with perhaps the three most skilled living Native makers of birchbark canoes in North America, (left to right) Alec Ratt, Jim Jerome and John Ratt, all Lake Barrière Algonquin.

infectious diseases. *Tikinâgans* were made a little while after the baby was born, as so many children died within a short time of birth.

David's fifteen-year-old daughter died in childbirth. The missionary, realizing that a breech presentation might doom both mother and child, had advised the skilled midwife to cut the baby out rather than have both baby and mother die. The midwife called in witnesses and cut the baby out. Unfortunately, David's daughter died right away. The baby lived a while, then it too died.

In the early 1960s, David Makakons was living by himself in a cabin at the old settlement of Barrière. His wife had died not long before. He was hard of hearing and nearly blind. He built several canoes a season despite his poor vision. He was fresh of mind and always busy with

David Makakons carving canoe ribs and his wife with their 2-day-old baby in a tikinâgan, Lake Barrière, 1929.

some work. One woman remembered that when she visited once, David paddled over to the old graveyard near the abandoned Hudson's Bay Company post to tend the graves. When he returned some time later, he had spruce roots and birchbark rolled up in the canoe.

He died in the summer of 1964, probably of a heart attack, after having fallen from the birchbark canoe he had used for four decades. He is buried in the old graveyard at Barrière.

According to Lina Nottaway, David Makakons never asked other Indians for money for a birchbark canoe. David would say to them, "If you see me doing something sometime, help me."

CHAPTER 17

There was much to learn from the Indians. Many things often appeared simple in retrospect. But that is just the point: looking back, we think they are very simple, but we'd be hard put to think of them on our own. Putting wood around a campfire to dry before tossing it in the fire is an obvious thing, but if you don't think of it, a fire becomes just that much harder to sustain.

On one occasion, Ernestine remained at our cabin, and I went to get canoe bark with Jim Jerome and two of his friends from Rapid Lake. We cut down a tree, harvested the bark, and then stopped for a lunch that consisted of moose meat fried in a pan and bannock that Jim's wife Angèle had made that morning in Rapid Lake. One of the other men, Pierre Ratt, who is also a birchbark canoe builder, cut a small dead spruce pole into two-foot lengths. He made a hot fire very quickly, and because he had put one layer of spruce sticks down and then the next layer cross-wise, the result was a grill on which the frying pan sat quite level.

I had been wearing holes through my moccasins and was becoming annoyed at having to put newspapers in the bottoms to plug the holes. I asked a Rapid Lake woman what to do. Did the Indians have any way to keep from wearing holes in the bottoms of moccasins? Millennia of dealing with footwear must surely have given them some insight.

"Yes," she replied patiently, "pick up your feet."

Earning money while living in the woods was not easy, and sometimes we were obliged to leave the cabin and go afield to make some money.

I had worked in the lumber camp at Ottawa Lake years before, and knew that there was money to be made at that arduous labour.

A friend of mine, who I knew made a good income, worked for a jobber. "You think he'd put on a new fellow?" I asked him.

"There's a good chance," he answered.

The next day I drove out in the woods several miles to where the gang was cutting. My friend had already spoken to the boss, so he was expecting me. "Just go next to André in the bush over there and start cutting four-footers."

Walking in the woods over a cushion of spruce branches was difficult; I was out of shape. I cut the first tree down, then, working from the butt end toward the top, sawed the branches off, being careful to avoid kickback. About every four feet, I cut a log.

After half an hour of sweating profusely, I realized that I had not asked the boss what he was going to pay. When I broached the subject he said, "Keep on working, you'll get paid what you're worth."

"I'm sorry," I said, laying the saw down. "I can't work for that; I have a wife to support."

◆

At the end of July when our anniversary approached, we decided to celebrate it with a canoe trip. The year before, we had taken our honeymoon in our birchbark canoe on Lake Superior.

The author portaging a birchbark canoe near Lake Samart, Quebec.

We took out a map and traced a route suggested by a friend who is a timber cruiser. He thought highly of Lake Cawasachouane, which he said was a beautiful lake near Grand Lake Victoria. Nearly all lakes in the area were potentially good for fishing, but we did not want other people on the same lake if this was going to be a first anniversary celebration.

Fishermen generally don't portage into isolated lakes, so we picked out little Lake Henault not far from Cawasachouane, as we had discovered the latter lake had road access.

We put the birchbark canoe in the water at Lake Henault. At the falls were two Indian cabins, though they were unoccupied when we passed. I took a special interest in them because I had been told by Father Edmond Brouillard, the Oblate missionary for the Grand Lake Victoria and Lake Simon Algonquin bands, that one of the cabins belonged to a Grand Lake Victoria Algonquin named Joe Gunn. Father Brouillard told me that Joe Gunn was in his fifties and was a skilled craftsman who made *tikinâgans* and wood and canvas canoes. That led me to believe that he could probably build birchbark canoes. All the signs were good: he was an Algonquin from an isolated area, over fifty, and he could build canvas canoes.

We had an easy paddle down Lake Henault. A black duck flew over us, quacking like a mallard. The shore of the lake was either boggy or rocky and brushy, and it would have been hard to find a place for our tent.

When we reached the end of Lake Henault, we found a portage to Padoue Lake. The portage was not as good as it could have been, but, at only two hundred yards, it was easily passable.

We entered Lake Padoue on a stream that had rocks, grass, and lily pads — fine habitat for northern pike. We paddled out into the lake, and then saw our spit of land. Padoue was graced with many beaches; one of them was on the spit. We pulled the birchbark canoe up on the beach and removed our dunnage.

There were blueberries behind the beach, but they were small and sparse. In western Quebec, it is either feast or famine as far as blueberries go. There is either not enough to put in a pancake or an astonishing quantity of them.

We set up our tent, unrolled our sleeping bags, and laid out the things for supper. Just then, we heard a great amount of splashing on the other side of the spit – obviously a moose – but we didn't go to investigate.

The next morning, we rose and went swimming right in front of the tent. One of the fine things about Canadian wilderness lakes is that if you are swimming and you become thirsty, you just open your mouth. Breakfast was Red River cereal, a Canadian staple of three whole grains. We fished in Padoue that day, and, in under twenty minutes, Ernestine neatly caught a northern pike of about three pounds and two walleyes of about a pound each.

When we went back to the campsite on the spit of land, Ernestine took a book into the tent to read. I had a book entitled *Children of the Sun* about Indian children and their milieu. I took the book and a jar of tea, paddled out in the birchbark canoe, and read for an hour and a half. The sun was warm and there was hardly any wind. The sky was a little hazy; there were forest fires in Manitoba and northern Ontario.

Late that afternoon we celebrated our anniversary in the most fitting way, by floating out and making love in the canoe. What can be more natural than doing the most natural act in the most natural of canoes? The only problem I can report is that things are a little difficult when a thwart is between you and your love.

The anniversary supper was elegant, I thought, for a meal in the woods. I did the honours. We had packed some shrimp and scallops – a couple of Ernestine's favourites – from Maniwaki. I fried them in garlic butter and the walleye in bacon grease. On the side were home fries and onions, and the whole was washed down with brandy. The feast was similar to the one we had had on our wedding trip to Lake Superior a year before.

The next morning we broke camp. When we arrived at Lake Henault we swam, as the portage had been a sweaty one. Down the lake, we came to a bay that was about a half a mile wide. There we saw a moose feeding on lily pads. We decided to sneak up on the moose by paddling behind a point.

It was near the end of July, so the moose had a good rack. We came within a hundred feet of him, but with the wind at our backs, it didn't take him long to discover us. As we continued to move silently toward him, he looked at us, harrumphed a few times, and walked into the bush.

◆

Back on the highway, I suggested to Ernestine that, rather than hurry south to our cabin we jog north a bit to Lake Simon and see if Father Brouillard was home.

The good father was glad to see us and put the tea kettle on immediately. That promised a long conversation.

"How long have you been at Grand Lake Victoria and Lake Simon?" I asked him. The community at Lake Simon was actually kind of an offshoot of the one at Grand Lake Victoria, a few hundred Algonquin from Grand Lake Victoria having been moved to Lake Simon just after the turn of the century.

"It will be twenty-five years soon," he said. He was an intelligent, though quiet-spoken man. "I was a year in northern Ontario, at Ogoki, before that to learn Ojibway."

He was born in the Lake St. Jean area north of Quebec City. He finished college at St. Laurent College in Montreal and then studied theology at the University of Ottawa.

I was truly curious about his connection with the Algonquin

language. "Do you preach in the language; do you read books in the language?"

"I preach in church in Algonquin. I work on liturgical texts, translations of the Bible. In the church, the readings are still in Algonquin, though with the young people you have to add English or French, depending on where you are. At the moment, I'm working on a study of the roots of the Algonquin language from the cultural point of view."

"Do you say Mass at Grand Lake Victoria and at Lake Simon only in Algonquin?" I asked. By now, we'd become so involved in the conversation that it was Ernestine who rose to refill the tea cups.

"About three-quarters in Algonquin, though with the young, a lot of French has to be added."

"Do you read in Algonquin regularly, as a person reads in French or English?"

"Yes," Father Brouillard said, "I read regularly in Algonquin. But the books we have are mostly liturgical."

"What is the best way to learn Algonquin?" I asked.

"I began when I went to Ogoki in northern Ontario. For two months, I was with another missionary who knew the language. We met each morning for one hour. He explained the grammar to me, and then he told me to practise with the Indians. So I went out hunting and trapping with them, especially with those who did not speak any English, the older people. They explained certain words to me by gestures, and they told me to write it down in my notebook. To get along a little bit in the language, it took four months. To feel comfortable, it took at least three years."

"What is the level of your ability today?" I asked. It was strange, but we were talking about an important intellectual discipline that was almost totally foreign to the Canadian school system at the secondary and university level. So much for a literate populace.

"I get along rather well in Algonquin," Father Brouillard said, as he sipped his tea. I knew he was being modest; with an Indian woman from Lake Simon he had put together a grammar of Algonquin. He continued: "There is always something to learn; some nuances that escape me, nuances in vocabulary. Another thing that happens is that, because it is an oral language, there are certain expressions that one family employs that another does not. There is always an adaptation to make. I work on three reserves. Grand Lake Victoria and Lake Simon are more or less the same family. But I go to Rapid Lake and there are other expressions and another way of thinking."

"Among the Indians at Grand Lake Victoria, how many speak English or French?" I wondered.

"As a second language, the majority of Indians at Grand Lake Victoria speak French," he said. "Perhaps 60 percent speak French."

"Therefore," I pointed out, "there must be 40 percent that speak only Algonquin."

"Yes, there is a good number, especially the old people. Among those who speak only Algonquin, there are some who understand a little French. But they will answer in Algonquin."

"Are there any living birchbark canoe makers at Grand Lake Victoria or at Lake Simon?"

"I don't know of any at Lake Simon or at Grand Lake Victoria, only at Rapid Lake. Here at Lake Simon, there was Basil Pokashish, who made some in the past; though I never saw him make one. He died today [sic!]. He was in his eighties."

"What was Patrick Maranda like when he was young?"

Father Brouillard smiled with affectionate memory. "He liked to speak about Indian culture very much. He liked to talk not only about birchbark canoes, but about other things. He liked to laugh and to tell stories. He was always doing something with his hands. He always had his crooked knife in his hands. He made snowshoes and *tikinâgans* in the winter and in the summer he made canoes behind his house."

He said that there might be someone at Grand Lake Victoria who could make a birchbark canoe, "among the old people. They have seen it. But they don't make them today. They're lacking practice. They make snowshoes and they repair canvas canoes with their crooked knives. The Gunns make canvas canoes; the grandmother makes birchbark baskets. They have nothing made ahead of time, but they welcome people. They're very hospitable people.

"The majority of the Grand Lake Victoria people spent the greatest part of the year in the woods. The old people and the young couples as well. They like to trap and spend their winters there. There are some at Lake Joncas, Lake Chartier, Trout Lake near Belleterre, and at Temiskaming. Across the woods, it's close to Grand Lake Victoria."

"Do the Indians at Grand Lake Victoria still have a good knowledge of Indian medicine?" I asked.

"There is still a little Indian medicine; they make a lot of infusions to help their health."

It seemed to me that Grand Lake Victoria was a special place. Life continued there in a very basic way that made it different from the other reserves. I asked Father Brouillard about this. Would the Algonquin remain at Grand Lake Victoria for a long time to come?

"It will be there for a long time. The people are very attached to the place. They like it very much.

"Grand Lake Victoria is a different place. First of all, it is isolated. To get there, you need a canoe. There is no electricity or running water. So it creates another way of thinking. And then the majority of the Indians spend the winter on their hunting grounds and in the summer they like to get together. It's a little like life in the past. To trap and then to get together in the summer to rest up. That differs very much. In large part, they continue as they did long ago.

"At Grand Lake Victoria, they have remained a trapping society. They still live in the woods. They like to hunt a lot. Even young children

Algonquin babies in their tikinâgans at Grand Lake Victoria in 1907.

have ability. Children of four or five will get in a canoe easily, whereas a young child here does not have the same adroitness in getting in a canoe. At Grand Lake Victoria, they use fibreglass and canvas canoes. They are equipped to live in the woods. They make hide vests, moccasins, and mittens, and they wear them. They have kept their ancestral culture; they have built log cabins. They live a nomadic life; they are not obliged to live at the village. And there is no school there. The children at Grand Lake Victoria love fishing. They can play at it all day. The people live on fish and on moose hunting. In the winter, they eat beaver.

"Grand Lake Victoria has remained the most isolated of the Algonquin reserves because it takes a canoe to get there."

We rose – eventually – and thanked Father Brouillard for the tea and for the time.

As we drove through the woods toward the main road, we spoke about Grand Lake Victoria. The name of Grand Lake Victoria had itself always had a magic to it. "Suppose," I asked Ernestine, "that we had a wide choice about learning to make a birchbark canoe. Where would we have gone and when?"

I think she may have been thinking the same thing as I, but it was I who voiced the thought:

"How about a hundred years ago at Grand Lake Victoria, when Christopherson was there and everyone spoke Algonquin, and the big fur trade canoes came and went every day, and we could have worked with the old canoe makers?"

EPILOGUE

Mary Commanda had a dream: if she won the lottery, she'd build an old folks' home on the reserve in Maniwaki.

Mary died several years ago. She never lived to win the lottery or to see the home that was built for the old people on the reserve.

After Mary's death, William and his brother-in-law Basil, who had been rooming and boarding with Mary and William for decades, moved from the busy road where they'd been living to the tranquillity of beautiful Bitobi Lake on the reserve.

Ernestine and I visited the recently constructed old folks' home. We knew the three staff members. They seemed particularly appreciative that we would come to visit the old people, and always served us tea.

I had noticed that the Indians, especially the older ones, frequently used the phrase "the old people" when talking about the elders. They seemed to have a special esteem for them.

The home for the elderly on the reserve was a modern, quiet place. The television was never on. An old man worked in his room with his crooked knife. The Rapid Lake Indians sometimes brought fish.

This is not to say that the transition to an old folks' home is a happy one. How can it be? It can be, obviously, a very stark *face à face* with one's own mortality. The majority of people only leave such places in a casket.

I'm not sure who convinced Basil that he needed to go to the old folks' home on the reserve, or why. Maybe it was the doctor who came regularly.

That summer, Basil had made three full-size birchbark canoes with his nephew Daniel. They were very good canoes, Basil's best. Daniel was an exceptionally good student. He paid great honour to Basil – not to mention to Jocko and to the other departed Algonquin canoe makers – by working hard and learning well.

But Basil was now eighty-two years old. At the end of the summer's building, his legs were very tired. Working with Daniel, he'd continued as he always had – sitting on a stump to carve with his crooked knife, kneeling on the ground to sew the gunwale with spruce root.

Was it this difficulty in walking that led the doctor to convince Basil to go to the old folks' home? I don't know. I do know that it was a big decision for Basil.

His great joy in life had been a very simple thing: to go where he wanted to go. With Jocko he trapped in the fall, made canoes in the summer; and guided for fishing and hunting at Désert Lake.

I am thankful that I was not present when Basil had to go to the old folks' home. I have trouble enough wrestling with the prospect of my own mortality. Basil's departure from William's house on Bitobi Lake – certainly a one-way trip – would have left me in a bad way emotionally had I been there at the time.

Basil had to make that final journey to the old folks' home – that had been decided. His friend Frank brought his pickup to William's house to load up Basil's things. They put several cardboard boxes on the back of the truck.

The sun was setting. William watched with sadness as Frank's truck left. He would see Basil again, of course; the home was only a few miles away. But William knew, as Basil knew, that going to a home for the aged was a kind of rupture from life.

William went back in the house and sat down on the sofa to read. I have no idea what his thoughts may have been regarding Basil's departure, but I can surmise. Basil was eighty-two; William eighty. Basil's going to the old folks' home represented something that we all must face.

About forty-five minutes later, William heard a truck pull up. He went to the window. It was Basil and Frank. William walked out on the porch.

Basil got out of the truck. He went in the back, picked up the first cardboard box and walked toward William on the porch.

As he mounted the steps with the box, Basil looked at William and said, speaking of the old folks' home, "I didn't care for it."

ALSO BY DAVID GIDMARK

Gidmark, David. *Building a Birchbark Canoe: The Algonquin Wâbanäki Tcîmân.*
    Mechanicsburg, Pennsylvania: Stackpole Books, 1994.
        Given here are the history of and general construction methods for
    the Algonquin birchbark canoe. The book describes birchbark canoe
    construction by Jocko Carle, William Commanda, James Jerome, and
    Daniel Sarazin. Included are an extensive glossary of Algonquin canoe
    terms and a good bibliography of the Algonquin nation.

The Indian Crafts of William and Mary Commanda. Mechanicsburg,
    Pennsylvania: Stackpole Books, 1995.
        In this book, the Commandas's methods for making of snowshoes,
    moccasins, cradleboards, wooden spoons, and a birchbark canoe are
    described.

"Building an Algonquin Birchbark Canoe." Trust for Native American
    Cultures and Crafts, 1984. Video, 52 minutes. Available from David
    Gidmark, Box 26, Maniwaki, Quebec J9E 3B3. Rental: US/Can$2.50;
    purchase: US$100.
        This video shows the birchbark canoe building process of Jocko
    Carle and Basil Smith. Made in 1980 when both men were in their
    early seventies, it is an excellent memorial to them.

*David and Ernestine Gidmark offer a summer birchbark canoe building course on the
Wisconsin shore of Lake Superior. For more information, please write them at Box 26,
Maniwaki, Quebec J9E 3B3, Canada.*

PHOTO CREDITS

Opening page, courtesy Edmond Brouillard, O.M.I., Lake Simon, Quebec:
p. v, courtesy Claude Nault, 1985: p. 10, Public Archives Canada: p. 18,
courtesy Edmond Brouillard, O.M.I., Lake Simon, Quebec: p. 19,
Smithsonian Institution: p. 20, courtesy Richard Nash: p. 23, Viking Ship
Museum, Roskilde, Denmark: p. 28, The Mariners' Museum, Newport
News, Virginia: p. 31, The Mariners' Museum, Newport News, Virginia:
p. 59, courtesy of the Museum of the American Indian, Heye Foundation,
1979: p. 85, courtesy of Désert Lake Fish and Game Club: p. 86, courtesy
of Désert Lake Fish and Game Club: p. 143, by Frederick Johnson, 1929,
courtesy of the Museum of the American Indian, Heye Foundation:
p. 145, Leonard Lee Rue III, 1959: p. 147, courtesy Claire Poirier: p. 177,
courtesy Elizabeth Maranda: p. 178, courtesy Bill Mason: p. 180, Ernestine
Gidmark, 1992: p. 181, Frederick Johnson, 1929, courtesy of the Museum
of the American Indian, Heye Foundation: p. 184, Ernestine Gidmark,
1989: p. 191, National Museums of Canada.

All other photographs by David Gidmark.

INDEX